Bocas del Toro
PANAMA
Travel Guide

Unlock Hidden Gems, Must-See Sights,
Adventures, and Thrilling Experiences

Cori J. Smith

D1522065

Copyright© Cori J. Smith 2024

Table of Contents

Scan the QR Code to view and navigate the map of Bocas

To Scan the QR Code:
1. Open your smartphone's camera app.
2. Point the camera at the QR code.
3.Hold the phone steady until it focuses on the code.
4. A notification or a pop-up should appear with the QR code's content.
5. Tap on the notification or follow the prompt to view the content or take action.

INTRODUCTION

Bocas del Tor o, a natural wonderland on the northern coast of Panama's Caribbean Sea, is one of Panama's most popular attractions. Bocas del Toro province extends from the Talamanca mountain system, which contains one of Central America's largest main cloud forests. The Bocas del Toro islands, home to Panama's first marine national park, have been designated as part of UNESCO's World Network of Biosphere Reserves. Bocas has a large and diversified ecology, ranging from cloud rainforests to lowland mangroves and islets.

The Bocas archipelago is made up of nine main island islets. Bocas del Toro is regarded as one of Panama's best ecotourism destinations, with visitors having access to an unlimited number of ecotourism-related activities. Bocas del Toro, dubbed the "Galapagos of the Caribbean," is one of the world's most biologically diverse areas. Bocas is America's most popular ecotourism destination due to its diverse geography and natural life. Bocas del Toro is more than just a beach resort, and with a little knowledge, you can discover all of its charms. More than 95% of the coral species found in the Caribbean Sea live in the waters surrounding the archipelago, and over 32 animals have been identified on the Bocas islands alone. It is not surprising that the Smithsonian Tropical Research Institute has a research station here.

Welcome to Bocas del Toro, where the vibrant colors of the Caribbean blend with Panama's lush vegetation. As you begin your journey to Bocas del Toro, be ready to be fascinated by its charming appeal and limitless opportunities for adventure. This hidden jewel has something for

everyone, whether you want to relax on pristine beaches, participate in exhilarating water sports, or immerse yourself in culture. Imagine coming off the boat on Isla Colón, Bocas del Toro's main island, and being met by a pleasant air scented with saltwater and coconut palms. The rhythmic beat of reggae music fills the air, enticing you to calm down, unwind, and enjoy the island's laid-back atmosphere. Explore the streets of Bocas Town, the archipelago's thriving capital, where colorful wooden buildings line the coast and vibrant shops sell exotic fruits and handmade goods. As you travel deeper into the heart of Bocas del Toro, you will come across a world of natural wonders waiting to be discovered.

Dive into crystal-clear waters teeming with marine life, snorkel alongside stunning sea turtles, or catch waves at world-class surf spots. Explore Bastimentos Island's deep rainforest, where hidden waterfalls, winding hiking trails, and elusive creatures await around every turn. But perhaps the actual enchantment of Bocas del Toro comes in its people, who are friendly, inviting, and proud of their rich cultural past. Start a conversation with a local craftsman at a roadside shop, learn to dance to the enticing rhythms of calypso music, or eat with a family in an indigenous community. In Bocas del Toro, every meeting provides an opportunity to connect with the destination's heart and spirit.

As you read through the pages of this guide, allow yourself to be carried away by the spirit of adventure and discovery that awaits you in Bocas del Toro. Whether you're a seasoned traveler or starting out on your first trip abroad, we've selected the ideal mix of practical information, insider tips, and local insights to help you make the most of your time in this tropical paradise. So pack your bags, leave your problems behind, and prepare to be captivated by the charm of Bocas del Toro, where every sunset is a masterpiece, every wave a symphony, and every minute an amazing journey. Welcome to Paradise. Welcome to Bocas del Toro.

Why Visit Bocas del Toro?

Imagine waking up to the gentle lapping of waves on the shore, the warm embrace of the sun on your skin, and the promise of boundless discovery spread out before you. That is the enchantment of Bocas del Toro: a location where time appears to pause, allowing you to fully immerse yourself in the beauty of your surroundings. But what makes Bocas del Toro genuinely unique? Let's take a look at why this enchanting place should be at the top of your vacation bucket list:

1. Outstanding Natural Beauty: Bocas del Toro has some of the most stunning natural beauty you've ever seen. From the beautiful beaches of Isla Colón to the clear waters of Bastimentos Island, every piece of this archipelago is a postcard-worthy paradise. Dive beneath the surface to see a variety of aquatic life, snorkel amid beautiful coral reefs, or simply enjoy nature's beauty at its best.

2. Rich Cultural Tapestry: Beyond its natural charms, Bocas del Toro is home to a diverse range of cultures and traditions. With influences from Afro-Caribbean,

Indigenous, and European past, Bocas del Toro's cultural richness is very intriguing. Explore Bocas Town's vibrant streets, enjoy flavorful native cuisine, and immerse yourself in the rhythms of local music and dancing.

3. Endless adventure awaits: Bocas del Toro is an adventure playground for both thrill seekers and nature enthusiasts. Surf the famed surf of Wizard Beach, climb through lush jungles in search of hidden waterfalls, or kayak along mangrove-lined waterways rich in wildlife. Bocas del Toro has enough thrill for adrenaline junkies and nature lovers both.

4. Escape to Island Time: Life in Bocas del Toro goes at its own pace, with a laid-back rhythm that encourages you to slow down, relax, and enjoy every moment. Whether you're lazing on a hammock on a secluded beach, enjoying a refreshing drink at a beachside bar, or simply watching the sunset paint the sky in pink and orange, time seems to have no meaning in this lovely island paradise.

5. A warm welcome awaits: Last but not least, the inhabitants of Bocas del Toro are among the most friendly and cordial you'll ever encounter. From the time you arrive, you will be greeted with smiles, hospitality, and a genuine feeling of community. Whether you're chatting with locals at a coastal cafe or dancing the night away at a boisterous fiesta, you'll feel completely at home in Bocas del Toro.

Bocas del Toro is a location unlike any other, where natural beauty, rich culture, adventure, and leisure combine to create an experience that will stay with you long after you return home. So, why should you visit Bocas del Toro? The fundamental question is: why wait any longer? Begin organizing your trip to this tropical paradise immediately, and prepare for the adventure of a lifetime. Come with us on a trip through time and culture as we discover Bocas del Toro together. From ancient traditions to modern marvels, the charms of this fascinating island are waiting to be discovered. Are you ready for the trip of a lifetime?

CHAPTER ONE

Discover Bocas del Toro

Welcome to the first chapter of your tour through Bocas del Toro, where we'll look at the fascinating geography, history, and colorful culture that have molded this stunning archipelago into the paradise it is today. We'll also examine the diverse routes to get to this paradise and stories from locals. Prepare to embark on a journey through time to discover the hidden stories and cultural treasures that await you in Bocas del Toro.

Geography and Climate

Bocas del Toro is a group of islands off Panama's northern Caribbean coast, roughly 9.3404° N latitude and 82.2501° W longitude. The archipelago is known for its pristine beaches, crystal-clear oceans, and deep tropical rainforests, making it a paradise for nature lovers and adventurers alike.
The climate in Bocas del Toro is tropical, with warm temperatures all year and distinct rainy and dry seasons. The dry season normally lasts from December to April, with

sunny days and calm seas perfect for beachgoers and outdoor activities. The wet season, which lasts from May to November, offers intermittent rain showers and thunderstorms, resulting in lush green landscapes and reprieve from tropical heat. Despite the occasional rain, Bocas del Toro is a gem that may be explored year-round. Whether you're lazing in the sun on a secluded beach, hiking through deep forest paths, or diving into the beautiful underwater world of coral reefs, there are plenty of opportunities for adventure in this tropical paradise.

When traveling through Bocas del Toro, take light clothing, swimsuits, sunscreen, and insect repellent to keep comfortable in the island's warm and humid atmosphere. Don't forget to bring your spirit of adventure and curiosity as we explore the wonders of this enchanting destination.

So grab your hat, and sandals, and prepare to go on an incredible tour through Bocas del Toro's breathtaking scenery and rich culture. This tropical paradise has something for everyone, whether you want to relax, go on an adventure, or learn about the local culture.

History & Culture

Bocas del Toro has a rich and diverse history, just like its natural beauty. For ages, the indigenous Ngäbe-Buglé and Naso tribes have lived on these islands, in harmony with the land and sea. Their habits, traditions, and spiritual practices, which are still in use today, demonstrate their strong connection to the natural environment.

In the 16th century, European adventurers were enticed to the coasts of Bocas del Toro by reports of gold and wealth. The Spanish conquistadors sought to settle the islands but were greeted with ferocious indigenous opposition. Over their attempts, the Ngäbe-Buglé and Naso tribes were resilient, sustaining their way of life over overwhelming odds.

Throughout colonial times, Bocas del Toro became a cultural melting pot, with settlers arriving from Spain, England, France, and the Caribbean in quest of opportunities. The islands' strategic location along Caribbean trade routes made them a commercial and trading hotspot, attracting merchants, pirates, and adventurers from all over the world. The architecture, gastronomy, and culture of Bocas del Toro continue to reflect this rich background. From the colorful wooden buildings of Bocas Town to the aromas of Caribbean-inspired cuisine, centuries of cultural interchange have permeated the archipelago's daily life.

Bocas del Toro began to gain popularity among travelers looking for sun, sand, and adventure in the late twentieth century. Bocas del Toro's gorgeous beaches, crystal-clear oceans, and thick rainforests captivated travelers from all over, making the island a sought-after haven. Tourism now plays an important part in Bocas del Toro's economy, giving jobs and opportunities for locals while also generating much-needed income to support conservation initiatives and community development. However, the islands are still devoted to sustainable tourism practices, conserving their natural beauty for future generations to enjoy.

As you visit Bocas del Toro, you will come across a vibrant tapestry of cultures and traditions that reflect the archipelago's diverse history. From the rhythmic sounds of Afro-Caribbean music to the colorful celebrations of local festivals, every area of Bocas del Toro is alive with energy and life. Take a trip through Bocas Town to experience the busy ambiance of the local markets, where sellers sell fresh vegetables, handicrafts, and souvenirs. Alternatively, travel to the islands' interior and visit indigenous villages to learn about historic traditions and practices passed down through generations.

As you learn more about Bocas del Toro's history and culture, you will get a greater understanding of its people's perseverance and spirit. Bocas del Toro is a destination where the past and present meet in a celebration of life, culture, and environment, from the indigenous tribes who have lived here for generations to modern-day explorers who call the islands home.

Getting to Panama City

I've been to Bocas del Toro several times and will assist you in locating the best method to get there so you can organize your trip with ease. From aircraft to buses and shuttles, let's dive straight into all your alternatives for getting to Bocas del Toro from Panama City.

The first step in traveling to Bocas del Toro from the United States or Canada is to fly into Panama City's Tocumen Airport. This is the most common route to arrive in Panama, and it applies whether you travel directly from Miami, New York, or Toronto. From Panama City, you can fly domestically to Bocas del Toro Isla Colón International Airport, take a bus, or use a shuttle. When you're in Panama

City, you can choose to get into Bocas del Toro by flight, bus, or water taxi.

1. By flight: The best way to go to Bocas del Toro from Panama City is by plane. Air Panama flights last 50 minutes and start at USD 70 each way. This is the simplest and most expensive alternative, but it is worthwhile to save time if it is within your budget. I flew to Bocas during my second trip to Panama. And, when flying in a tiny plane, it was amazing to see Bocas del Toro from above and remember some of the islands from my first visit.

Another option you can try is Lift Panama. They offer smaller plane options as well. You can also choose to fly out of Albrook Airport, which is a 40-minute Uber or taxi ride from Tocumen International Airport. Albrook is a domestic airport near Albrook Mall, but Tocumen is Panama City's main airport, so don't mix them up! If unsure, consider booking a shuttle service.

Insider tip: I'll advise you to plan to spend a night in Panama City before your journey. This ensures that any flight delays from outside of Panama do not lead you to miss a same-day domestic flight and it also gives you the time to explore the beauty of Panama City. You can spend your layover in Panama City exploring Casco Viejo, hiking in the city's parks, and visiting the iconic Panama Canal. Panama City offers a variety of enjoyable activities for visitors.

Tips for Flying to Bocas del Toro

- Book your flight as soon as you know the dates, as seats are limited.
- Checked bags are not included in the lowest flight price and are an additional tax. Please double-check your luggage size and add it to your flight ticket if necessary.
- To ensure a smooth check-in process, arrive one hour before your flight time. Arriving too early may result in a lack of seating.
- If you want to save money, travel to Bocas and then take the overnight bus back to Panama City.

2. By Bus: Taking the bus from Panama City is an inexpensive method to go to the islands. It bundles one night's lodging and transportation into one price. It takes about 10 to 12 hours for the Panama City night bus to get to Boca del Toro. The bus leaves Albrook Bus Terminal around 6 to 8 pm. Bus tickets can be purchased at the Albrook Bus Terminal on the day of travel for around USD 35.

The next morning, between 6 and 7:30 a.m., you'll arrive in Almirante and take a taxi to the port before taking a water taxi to Bocas del Toro. Don't worry, taxis are always waiting for the night bus to arrive, so you may continue your journey even if you're half asleep like I was.

Taxis in Almirante (from 1 USD, 5-minute journey) and water taxis (from $6, 20-minute ride) are not included in the price of your bus ticket.

Tips for Taking the Bus to Bocas del Toro

- Arrive early at the bus terminal to buy your same-day ticket and reserve your spot.
- Bring a travel blanket or wear a sweater and slacks as buses are strongly air-conditioned, making it difficult to sleep when cold.
- Pack light for simpler travel on buses and water taxis.

Whatever option you select, it will be an experience! I've taken many ways to Bocas on previous visits. I've flown, riding a bus, a shuttle, and a boat ride; I've seen it all!

Local Voices

During my vacation in Bocas del Toro, I took my time to study some of the locals' way of life. My friends and I went further to interview them on what makes Bocas del Toro special and why they prefer to reside in the area. In this section, I'll introduce you to some of the remarkable people who call Bocas del Toro home, giving their distinct viewpoints, insider recommendations, and poignant experiences to help you better appreciate this magical place.

Meet **Maria**, a native Bocas del Toro inhabitant whose family has resided there for generations. As we sit on her front porch, viewing the crystal-clear seas, Maria expresses her love for her hometown and provides vital insights into the local way of life. "Growing up in Bocas del Toro has been a blessing," Maria recalls, smiling. "We do not have much monetary richness, but we are wealthy in culture, community, and natural beauty. Every day, I'm grateful to be able to call this location home."

When asked about her favorite areas in Bocas del Toro, Maria immediately mentions Playa Estrella, often known as Starfish Beach, a quiet stretch of shoreline noted for its beautiful blue seas and abundance of starfish. "Starfish Beach holds a special place in my heart," Maria says. "My family and I used to spend lazy Sundays picnicking on the dunes and watching the sunset. It's a hidden gem that I enjoy sharing with people looking to discover the true essence of Bocas del Toro."

Next, meet **Carlos**, a local fisherman whose livelihood is reliant on the abundant seas surrounding the islands. As we board his boat for a morning fishing expedition, Carlos tells us about his sea adventures and the necessity of sustainable fishing tactics. "For us fishermen, the ocean is our lifeline," Carlos adds, his aged face furrowed with experience. "We have great regard for the sea and all of its inhabitants, and we seek to live in peace with nature. By using sustainable fishing practices, we ensure that future generations can continue to enjoy the sea's treasures."

Carlos' enthusiasm for his trade is obvious as he deftly navigates the sea, casting his net with accuracy and patience. As the sun rises over the horizon, bathing the sky in pink and gold, Carlos reflects on Bocas del Toro's everlasting beauty. "Every day on the water is a reminder of the awe-inspiring beauty of nature," Carlos says. "No matter how many times I see a sunrise or a pod of dolphins playing in the waters, it never fails to overwhelm me with awe and thankfulness. Bocas del Toro is a true paradise unlike any other."

Personal Stories

In addition to our interviews with locals, we've had the opportunity to hear personal experiences from those who have chosen to call Bocas del Toro home. These touching vignettes provide insight into the rich tapestry of lives that comprise the fabric of this close-knit community.

Alejandro, a transplanted artist from Argentina, tells his story of falling in love with Bocas del Toro's lively culture and breathtaking environment. Alejandro leads us through his colorful studio overlooking the sea, explaining how the beauty of the islands has inspired his artwork and enhanced his life in ways he never dreamed of.

"For me, Bocas del Toro is more than just a place - it's a muse," Alejandro says, gesturing to his colorful paintings that reflect the essence of island life. "The rhythm of the ocean, the vibrant colors of the Caribbean, the warmth of the people - all of these elements infuse my work with a sense of joy and vitality that I find truly inspiring."

Another account comes from **Marta,** a retired schoolteacher who relocated to Bocas del Toro in search of a slower pace of life and a stronger connection to nature. Marta thinks of the peace and serenity she has found in her new home as she tends to her lush garden, which is filled with tropical flowers and fruit trees.

"Living in Bocas del Toro has been a dream come true for me," Marta adds, her eyes beaming with happiness. "Every morning, I awaken to the sound of birdsong and the gentle rustle of palm trees in the breeze." It's a sensory wonderland, with each moment feeling like a gift."

As we say goodbye to Marta and the other locals who have generously shared their tales with us, we get a better respect for the beauty, friendliness, and tenacity of the people of Bocas del Toro. Their stories serve as a reminder that genuine wealth is found not in worldly items, but in the depth of human connection and the beauty of nature.

In the next sections of this tour, we'll look at some of the must-see sights, hidden gems, and local secrets that distinguish Bocas del Toro from other vacation destinations. So gather your spirit of adventure and prepare to explore the heart and soul of this tropical paradise.

CHAPTER TWO

Essential Information

Welcome to Chapter 2 of your Bocas del Toro Travel Guide, where we'll review the important details you should know before embarking on your tropical journey. We've got you covered on everything from monetary recommendations to language requirements.

Currency in Bocas del Toro

When planning a trip to Bocas del Toro, one of the first questions you'll want to ask is what currency to use. Panama's official currency is the Panamanian Balboa (PAB), so don't be concerned if you've never heard of it before. The US Dollar (USD) is Panama's de facto currency and is widely accepted in Bocas del Toro. Most costs are quoted in dollars, and you'll rarely have to exchange your currency for balboas.

When it comes to paying for products and services in Bocas del Toro, cash reigns, while credit cards are accepted by many restaurants, hotels, and tour operators, you should keep some cash on hand for minor purchases, street vendors, and tips. ATMs are widely available in Bocas Town and other popular tourist destinations, allowing you to withdraw dollars or balboas as needed.

Language in Bocas del Toro

Bocas del Toro's unique cultural past, as expressed in its language and customs, is one of its most distinguishing features. While Spanish is Panama's official language, English is frequently used in Bocas del Toro, particularly among tourists and the local expatriate community.

Don't worry if your Spanish is rusty; you'll be able to communicate with both natives and other travelers in English. Language difficulties are rare in Bocas del Toro, whether you're ordering a meal at a seaside café or chatting with a pleasant boat captain.

Of course, learning a few simple Spanish phrases can improve your experience and demonstrate respect for the local culture. So, why not practice a bit before your trip? Whether you're greeting someone with a cheerful "Hola" or buying a cool "cerveza" (beer) at a beach bar, knowing a few phrases of Spanish can help you connect with locals and immerse yourself in the lively culture of Bocas del Toro.

Tips for Confidently Navigating Bocas del Toro

Now that you're familiar with the money and language of Bocas del Toro, here are a few more pointers to assist you confidently navigate this tropical paradise:

- Exchange Some Cash: Although dollars are generally accepted in Bocas del Toro, it's always a good idea to keep some local money on hand for smaller purchases and emergencies. Dollars can be converted into balboas at banks and currency exchange bureaus in Bocas Town.

- Brush Up on Your Spanish: While English is widely spoken in Bocas del Toro, knowing some basic Spanish can enhance your experience and allow you to communicate with locals. Consider purchasing a language app or taking a crash course before your trip.

- Be Mindful of Cultural Differences: Bocas del Toro is a cultural melting pot with influences from Panama, the Caribbean, and beyond. Be respectful of local customs and traditions, and always obtain permission before photographing people or their property.

- Stay Safe and Hydrated: Bocas del Toro has a hot and humid climate, so drink plenty of water and apply sunscreen to protect yourself from the sun's rays. Keep your belongings safe and stay attentive to your surroundings, especially in crowded tourist locations.

Visa and Entry Regulations

Now that you're getting ready for your excursion, it's critical to grasp the visa requirements and entry restrictions to ensure a smooth and hassle-free trip.

One of the first tasks in organizing your vacation to Bocas del Toro is to determine whether you require a visa to enter Panama. The good news is that many countries' residents can visit Panama for short periods without requiring a visa. This includes travelers from the United States, Canada, the European Union, and many other countries.

- Visa-Free Entry: If you have a passport from a visa-exempt nation, you can visit Panama without a visa for up to 180 days. This flexible policy gives you plenty of time to discover the marvels of Bocas del Toro and beyond without having to secure a visa in advance.

- Tourist Card: Upon arrival in Panama, you must acquire a Tourist Card, also known as a Tarjeta de Turismo. This card costs USD 20 and is usable for stays of up to 30 days. You can acquire the Tourist Card at the immigration counter in the airport or port of entry, so make sure you have enough cash to cover the charge.

- Extension of Stay: If you fall in love with Bocas del Toro and wish to prolong your stay beyond the Tourist Card's original 30-day limit, you have options. You can apply for an extension of stay at the National Immigration Service offices in Bocas del Toro and Panama City. Extensions are normally given in 30-day increments, with a maximum of 180 days total.

Visa requirements for other nationalities: While many people have visa-free access to Panama, it is critical to check the visa requirements for your nationality before traveling. Citizens of some countries may be required to obtain a visa or other papers to enter Panama, so do your homework ahead of time to prevent any surprises.

Entry Regulations and Customs

In addition to visa requirements, it is critical to become acquainted with Panama's entrance restrictions and customs procedures to guarantee a pleasant arrival experience. Here are some important considerations to bear in mind:

- Passport Validity: Your passport should be valid for at least six months after your intended departure from Panama. Check the expiration date of your passport well in advance of your trip and renew it if needed.

- Custom Declaration: Upon arrival in Panama, you must fill out a customs declaration form. This form requests basic information about you and any products you are bringing into the nation, including cash, gadgets, and personal belongings. To minimize any complications with customs officers, fill out the form honestly and accurately.

- Importation of certain products, such as firearms, drugs, and counterfeit goods, is strictly regulated in Panama. It is critical to become acquainted with the list of prohibited things to prevent any legal ramifications or confiscation of merchandise upon arrival.

- Health Declaration: Given current global health concerns, Panama may require tourists to sign a health declaration form upon arrival. This form often inquires about recent travel history, symptoms of disease, and contact with sick people. Prepare to deliver truthful and accurate facts to protect public health.

Understanding Panama's visa requirements and entry procedures can give you confidence and peace of mind while you travel to Bocas del Toro. Whether you're planning a brief vacation or a longer stay in paradise, understanding the intricacies of admission processes helps ensure a pleasant and flawless travel experience.

Getting Around Bocas del Toro

In this section, we'll go over the vital information you need to get around this tropical paradise with ease. Here, we will focus on transportation choices, ensuring that you can easily discover all that Bocas del Toro has to offer.

When you arrive at Bocas del Toro, you'll be ready to begin exploring the beautiful islands and colorful culture that await you. Fortunately, moving throughout this archipelago is simple, thanks to a multitude of transportation alternatives customized to each traveler's preferences.

1. Water Taxi: Water taxis are the lifeline of Bocas del Toro, connecting the islands with mainland locations. These

colorful boats may be seen stationed around the shoreline, waiting to transport you away on your next adventure. Whether you're traveling between islands or to a quiet beach, water taxis are a convenient and scenic option.

Tip: Before embarking on your excursion, negotiate the fee with the boat captain to guarantee you obtain the best price.

2. Bicycles: Bicycles are ideal for exploring Bocas del Toro at

a relaxed pace. Many establishments provide bike rentals, allowing you to explore the lovely streets of Isla Colón and beyond. Cycling is not only environmentally responsible, but it is also an excellent opportunity to immerse yourself in the island's natural beauty, thanks to bike-friendly paths and spectacular coastal vistas.

Tip: Keep a look out for bike rental outlets near your hotel, or ask the staff for recommendations.

3. Rental cars: If you prefer to explore at your leisure, hiring a car is a great way to move about Bocas del Toro. Isla

Colón has rental firms that offer a variety of vehicles to meet your needs, from modest cars to tough SUVs. With well-maintained roads and scenic drives, hiring a car allows you to get off the usual route and explore hidden jewels all across the archipelago.

Tip: Before you hit the road, make sure you're familiar with the local traffic regulations and circumstances.

4. ATVs & Golf Carts: Renting an ATV or golf cart is a fun and exciting way to explore Bocas del Toro. These off-road vehicles are an exciting kind of transportation, letting you speed across the islands and explore secluded beaches and jungle trails. Whether you're riding along sandy beaches or traversing tiny forest paths, an ATV or golf cart rental will provide a memorable island experience.

Tip: Remember to use sunscreen and protective gear, especially if you'll be riding in the sun for a long time.

5. Walking: Last but not least, don't overlook the pleasure of exploring Bocas del Toro on foot. Many attractions, restaurants, and stores are within walking distance of popular lodgings, making it simple to wander through the colorful streets and take up the laid-back vibe. Walking, whether along the waterfront or through colorful marketplaces, allows you to experience Bocas del Toro's charm up close and personal.

Tip: Wear comfortable shoes and bring a refillable water bottle to stay hydrated while exploring on foot.

If you are staying on Isla Colon, you can also rent an ATV, motor scooter, e-bike, or even a car. Below is a list of businesses that hire vehicles in Bocas Town:

- You can rent a car at Bocas del Toro Rent-a-Car
- Bocas E-Bikes offers E-bikes for rentals.
- Flying Pirates offers ATV rentals, e-bikes, and motor scooters.
- Boca Carts offers Golf Cart for rent.

Insider tips: Make sure to budget for both sea and land taxis. Inquire about your accommodation and how much it costs considering the distance of your accommodation to the area you intend to go. They usually bill every person and can get costly depending on how far you go, such as a $15 base fee to Bluff Beach or $8 a person to Red Frog Beach.

Make sure to collect some water taxi or land taxi numbers from your lodging. Everyone in Bocas del Toro uses WhatsApp, and you can text or phone any cab driver for free via WiFi. However, this perk is dependent on the hotel you're staying in.

Getting about Bocas del Toro, regardless of the means of transportation you use, will undoubtedly be an adventure. So take a water taxi, bicycle your way through paradise, or hit the road in a rented car; the options are limitless in this tropical paradise.

Safety and Health Recommendations

Safety Tips

First, let's talk about safety. While Bocas del Toro is generally a secure destination for tourists, you must take steps to safeguard yourself and your things. Below are some precautionary advice to keep in mind.

1. Stay Alert: Pay attention to your surroundings and trust your instincts. If something feels strange, do not hesitate to leave the situation.

2. Secure Your Belongings: Petty theft can occur, particularly in congested places and tourist sites. Keep your possessions near to you and avoid carrying big sums of cash or valuables.

3. Use Reliable Transportation: When going throughout the islands, choose trustworthy water taxi services and certified tour operators. Avoid traveling or accepting rides from strangers.

4. Swim Safely: While the waters around Bocas del Toro are magnificent, swimming, snorkeling, and surfing should be done with caution. Be aware of strong currents and listen to lifeguards' warnings.

5. Respect Wildlife: Bocas del Toro is home to a wide variety of species, including monkeys, sloths, and marine critters. Keep a secure distance and don't feed or pursue wild animals.

6. Drink responsibly: Having a tropical cocktail or two is part of the Bocas del Toro experience, but remember to drink sensibly. Pace yourself and avoid excessive alcohol consumption, especially if you intend to engage in water sports.

Health Advice

Now, let's speak about remaining healthy on your trip to Bocas del Toro. Here are some health suggestions to keep you feeling your best:

1. Protect your skin: The Caribbean sun can be fierce, so bring plenty of sunscreen with a high SPF. Reapply frequently, especially after swimming or sweating, and seek shade during the warmest hours of the day.

2. Stay hydrated: Bocas del Toro's warm heat and heavy humidity make it easy to become dehydrated. Drink plenty of water throughout the day to stay hydrated, especially if you spend time outside.

3. Preventing Mosquito Bites: While the risk of mosquito-borne illnesses is low in Bocas del Toro, you should nevertheless protect yourself against bites. Use DEET-based insect repellent, wear long sleeves and pants at dawn and dusk, when mosquitoes are most active, and consider staying in lodgings with screens or air conditioning.

4. Eat Fresh and Clean: Enjoy Bocas del Toro's great cuisine while being cautious of food safety. Choose restaurants and street vendors with strong hygiene standards, wash your hands frequently, and choose cooked items that are served hot.

5. Prepare a First Aid Kit: It is usually a good idea to keep a basic first aid kit available for minor injuries and illnesses. Bring bandages, antiseptic wipes, medications for pain relief, and any other personal meds you might need.

Following these safety recommendations and health advice will allow you to have a worry-free and happy experience in

Bocas del Toro. Now that you've prepared to be safe and healthy, it's time to embark on the adventures that await you in this tropical paradise!

CHAPTER THREE

Exploring Bocas del Toro

In this chapter, we'll delve into the variety of experiences that make visiting Bocas del Toro an amazing adventure. From pristine beaches to lush jungles, exhilarating water activities to cultural interactions, this tropical paradise has something for everyone to discover.

Top 11 Must-See Attractions

Bocas del Toro has some of the Caribbean's most magnificent attractions. Here are some must-see destinations that should be at the top of your itinerary:

1. Isla Colón

Isla Colón is the largest and most active island in the Bocas del Toro archipelago. With its beautiful beaches, rich rainforests, and lively atmosphere, Isla Colón is a must-see destination for travelers looking for a memorable Caribbean experience. Let's explore everything this tropical paradise has to offer.

Getting There

Traveling to Isla Colón is part of the journey. If you arrive by air, you will land at Bocas del Toro International Airport,

which is located on Isla Colón itself. From there, it's a quick taxi or water taxi ride to your hotel.

If you want a picturesque journey, you can take a boat from the mainland to Isla Colón. Regular water taxis depart from Almirante, the Bocas del Toro archipelago's gateway. Sit back, relax, and take in the breathtaking vistas as you ride across the crystal-clear waters toward your island paradise.

Exploring Isla Colón

Once you've landed on Isla Colón, it's time to explore. The following are some of the must-see sights and activities that await you:

- Playa Bluff: Begin your island experience by visiting Playa Bluff, one of Bocas del Toro's most stunning beaches. With its golden sands, blue waters, and towering palm trees, Playa Bluff is ideal for sunbathing, swimming, or simply relaxing and admiring the gorgeous environment. Bring lots of sunscreen and water, as there are minimal facilities on the beach.

- Bocas Town: No trip to Isla Colón is complete without visiting Bocas Town, the island's lively center. Here, you'll find colorful Caribbean-style buildings, busy clubs and restaurants, and an irresistible vibe. Take a walk along the waterfront, eat wonderful seafood at local restaurants, or browse the stores for souvenirs and handcrafted items.

- The Floating Bar: The Floating Bar is our top recommendation for must-see sights on Isla Colon. Take a $2/2-minute water taxi from Bocas Town to enjoy the fresh breeze, cold drinks, and delicious meals. It's a simple establishment, but it has everything you need: a welcoming and casual atmosphere, beers and margaritas, tacos, ceviches, and quesadillas. Swimming, snorkeling, Live Music on Mondays, and a diving board on the second floor allow you to perfect your belly flops after too many tequila shots! Open every day from December 1 to April 30.

- Bastimentos National Marine Park: Bastimentos National Marine Park, located just a short boat trip from Isla Colón, is a protected area rich in marine life and pristine coral reefs. Explore the park's mangrove forests, stroll through lush rainforests, or embark on a guided snorkeling tour to see the Caribbean Sea's undersea delights. Keep a lookout for colorful fish, marine turtles, and dolphins playing in the surf.

- Red Frog Beach: For a picture-perfect beach experience, visit Red Frog Beach on Isla Bastimentos. This lovely stretch of beach is well-known for its crystal-clear waters, smooth white sand, and unique red frogs that live there. Spend the day sunbathing, swimming, and snorkeling, or take a leisurely walk along the beach and keep an eye out for wildlife.

- Cocoa plantation Tour: Discover the island's rich history and culture by visiting a local cocoa plantation. Discover the ancient processes of cacao farming and chocolate production, from collecting cacao pods to grinding beans and creating delectable chocolate delicacies. Sample freshly baked chocolate treats and develop a new respect for this favorite tropical delicacy.

Creating Memorable Experiences

To make the most of your visit to Isla Colón, consider the following suggestions:

- Slow down, relax, and enjoy the laid-back atmosphere of island life. Take time to enjoy the simple pleasures, such as viewing the sunset over the water or sipping cocktails at a beachfront bar.
- Off the Beaten Path: While renowned sights such as Playa Bluff and Bocas Town are well worth a visit, don't be afraid to wander off the beaten path and uncover hidden beauties buried away in distant areas of the island.

- Respect the Environment: By practicing responsible tourism, you may help preserve Isla Colón's natural beauty for decades to come. Avoid pollution, respect wildlife and marine environments, and patronize environmentally friendly enterprises wherever feasible.
- Connect with Locals: Spend time chatting with locals and learning about their way of life. You'll be astounded by their kindness, hospitality, and genuine affection for their island home.

2. National Marine Park of Isla Bastimentos

Parque Nacional Marino Isla Bastimentos is a natural marine park tucked in the magnificent Bocas del Toro archipelago in Panama. If you're looking for a memorable vacation surrounded by breathtaking natural beauty, this ecological treasure is a must-see stop on your trip through paradise.

Exploring Marino National Park, Isla Bastimentos
As you arrive on the shores of Isla Bastimentos, you will be greeted by a lush tropical rainforest alive with wildlife. This

protected area covers more than 13,000 hectares of land and sea, making it one of Panama's largest marine parks. Parque Nacional Marino Isla Bastimentos, with its brilliant coral reefs and lush mangrove forests, is a haven for biodiversity and ecological conservation.

Scan to navigate the map of the National marine park

Getting There

Reaching the Parque Nacional Marino Isla Bastimentos is an experience in and of itself. The park is accessible by boat from the town of Bocas del Toro, where you can take a water taxi or a guided tour of the island. The trek takes about

20-30 minutes, and you may take in the stunning views of the surrounding archipelago along the way.

Must-See Attractions

When you get to Parque Nacional Marino Isla Bastimentos, you'll be spoiled for choice because there are so many sites to discover. Here are some of the must-see highlights that will make your visit to the park unforgettable:

- Red Frog Beach: Red Frog Beach, named after its resident amphibians, is a postcard-perfect paradise that exemplifies Isla Bastimentos' natural splendor. With immaculate white sand, crystal-clear waters, and lush tropical surroundings, this lovely beach is ideal for sunbathing, swimming, and snorkeling.

- Coral Reefs & Marine Life: Under the surface of the azure waters that surround Isla Bastimentos, there is a thriving underwater world filled with marine life. Snorkelers and scuba divers will be captivated by the vibrant coral reefs, unusual fish, and other fascinating animals that inhabit these waters. Keep a lookout for sea turtles, stingrays, and perhaps the elusive seahorse while exploring the park's rich marine habitat.

- Mangrove Forests & Wildlife: Explore the enchanting splendor of the mangrove trees that line the coastline of Isla Bastimentos. These distinct environments are home to a diverse range of fauna, including sloths, monkeys, and a stunning array of bird species. Take a guided kayak excursion through the mangroves to get up close and personal with the wildlife that inhabits this beautiful area.

- Wizard Beach: For those looking for a more remote and calm break, Wizard Beach provides a serene hideaway away from the rush and bustle of the main tourist destinations. To get there, use a trail from Bastimentos Town. It will take you around 20 minutes to get through the bush, giving you plenty of time to spot some wild animals along the route. Bring sturdy shoes, a hat, sunscreen, insect repellent, water, and something to eat for the hike. This isolated stretch of shoreline is ideal for beachcombing, beach yoga, or simply relaxing with the sounds of the sea and rustling palm palms. Wizard Beach is noted for its waves, which are great for surfing. However, when trekking, you must exercise caution and adequately preserve your possessions.

Creating Memorable Experiences

To get the most out of your visit to Parque Nacional Marino Isla Bastimentos, try some of the following activities that will immerse you in the area's natural beauty and cultural richness:

- Join a guided eco-tour conducted by qualified local guides who can explain the nature, history, and culture of Isla Bastimentos.
- Participate in a beach cleanup campaign to help preserve the unspoiled beauty of Red Frog Beach and other coastal regions in the park.
- Learn about the conservation work underway to safeguard the delicate ecosystems of Parque Nacional Marino Isla Bastimentos, as well as how you may help promote sustainable tourism practices.
- Spend the night under the stars in one of the park's eco-friendly lodges or campsites, falling asleep to the sounds of the jungle and waking up to the sunrise over the Caribbean Sea.

Parque Nacional Marino Isla Bastimentos is a wonderful gem of Bocas del Toro, providing visitors with a one-of-a-kind opportunity to connect with nature and explore Panama's Caribbean coast. Whether you're exploring the pristine beaches, snorkeling amid brilliant coral reefs, or trekking through the forest in search of animals, the park guarantees an incredible trip that will leave you with life-long memories. So pack your sense of adventure and travel to Parque Nacional Marino Isla Bastimentos, where paradise awaits.

3. Exploring Red Frog Beach

Red Frog Beach, located on the picturesque Isla Bastimentos in Bocas del Toro, is a slice of paradise that offers amazing experiences to every traveler. This magnificent beach, with its pristine white sands, crystal-clear seas, and thick jungle backdrop, exemplifies natural beauty and peace.

Getting there: The journey to Red Frog Beach is an adventure in and of itself. From the main island of Isla Colón, visitors can take a water taxi or book a boat cruise to Isla Bastimentos. The trek takes about 20-30 minutes and provides panoramic views of the Caribbean Sea along the route. As you approach Isla Bastimentos, you'll be greeted

by lush mangrove trees and colorful coral reefs, indicating your impending arrival at Red Frog Beach.

When you step onto the powdery shores of Red Frog Beach, you'll feel the cares of everyday life slip away. This beautiful beach, which stretches for over a mile along the island's coastline, is ideal for basking in the sun, relaxing with a good book, or simply admiring the breathtaking surroundings.

Unique Things to See and Do

While sitting on the beach and enjoying a refreshing plunge in the turquoise waters are unquestionably highlights of any

visit to Red Frog Beach, there are plenty of additional
activities to enjoy as well:

- Surfing: Red Frog Beach, with its steady waves and
  warm seas, is a surfers' paradise for all ability levels.
  Whether you're a seasoned pro or a beginner
  wanting to catch your first wave, there are lots of
  surf schools and rental shops that provide
  equipment and lessons.

- Hiking: For those seeking adventure, the
  neighboring rainforest has miles of trekking paths
  waiting to be explored. Take a stroll through the lush
  rainforest, keeping an eye out for colorful animals
  like monkeys, sloths, and unusual birds.

- Zip-lining: For a bird's-eye perspective of the island's
  breathtaking scenery, why not try zip-lining? Several
  tour providers provide thrilling zip-line trips into
  the rainforest canopy, with spectacular views and an
  adrenaline rush unlike any other.

- Snorkeling and Dive: Dive beneath the surface of
  the Caribbean Sea to explore a world of brilliant
  coral reefs, colorful fish, and fascinating aquatic life.
  Snorkeling and diving are popular activities at Red
  Frog Beach, with a variety of tour operators

providing guided tours to the top dive locations in the region.

- Turtle Watching: If you're lucky enough to arrive during the nesting season (March to October), you might be able to experience one of nature's most magnificent spectacles: sea turtle nesting and hatching. Join a guided turtle-watching excursion to see these magnificent creatures up close as they go from sea to shore.

Whether you're looking for adventure, leisure, or a chance to reconnect with nature, Red Frog Beach provides something for everyone. This tropical paradise, with its immaculate sands and crystal-clear waters, lush jungle environs, and abundance of wildlife, is sure to leave a lasting impact on everyone who visits.

4. Dolphin Bay

Welcome to Dolphin Bay, a hidden gem located among the gorgeous waters of Bocas del Toro. As you commence on your journey to this enchanting site, prepare to be captivated by the beauty of nature and the joyous spirits of its inhabitants, the dolphins.

Dolphin Bay is a quiet bay on the southeastern coast of Isla San Cristobal, one of the several islands that comprise the Bocas del Toro archipelago. What distinguishes this bay is its reputation as a haven for dolphins, who call the crystal-clear waters home. One of the biggest draws to Dolphin Bay is the opportunity to see these gorgeous creatures in their natural habitat. As you float across the tranquil seas in a boat or kayak, keep a lookout for playful dolphins gliding gently by you. Watch in astonishment as they leap and frolic in the surf, putting on an incredible spectacle that will take your breath away.

How to get there
Reaching Dolphin Bay is an adventure in itself. The majority of visitors choose to take a guided boat excursion from Bocas Town, the main focus of activities in Bocas del Toro. These tours usually include round-trip transportation, so you can sit back, relax, and take in the breathtaking landscape as you travel to Dolphin Bay.
Alternatively, you can rent a kayak and travel to Dolphin Bay at your own pace. This self-guided journey provides a more intimate experience, allowing you to connect with nature and enjoy the serene beauty of the surrounding mangroves.

Unique Things to See and Do

While Dolphin Bay is most famous for its resident dolphins, there is a lot more to see and do in this gorgeous setting:

- Snorkeling: Dive into Dolphin Bay's crystal-clear waters and experience a thriving underwater world alive with colorful coral reefs and tropical fish. Bring your snorkeling gear and discover the hidden gems beneath the surface.

- The Mangrove Tour: Join a guided mangrove tour and travel through narrow canals dotted with towering mangrove plants. Discover the mangroves' unique environment while spotting unusual birds, reptiles, and other species along the route.

- Beach Picnic: Pack a wonderful picnic lunch and spend the day relaxing on Dolphin Bay's gorgeous beaches. This isolated beach, with its pristine white beaches and swaying palm palms, is ideal for relaxation and sunbathing.

- Sunset Cruise: Wrap up your day in paradise with a romantic sunset boat around Dolphin Bay. Watch as the sky is painted orange and pink, giving a lovely glow over the tranquil waters underneath.

Tip for a Fun Experience

- Pack sunscreen, a hat, and lots of water to stay hydrated under the Caribbean sun.
- Respect the dolphins' natural habitat and observe them from a safe distance to prevent disrupting their surroundings.
- Bring a waterproof camera or GoPro to record special moments with the dolphins and other marine life.
- Reserve your boat trip or kayak rental in advance, especially during high tourist season, to ensure availability.

Dolphin Bay is more than simply a destination; it's a refuge where you can reconnect with nature, marvel at the beauty of the sea, and make memories that last a lifetime. So pack your spirit of adventure and travel to Dolphin Bay, where enchantment meets the sea and dreams come true.

Insider tip: You can take a tour with the Dolphin Bay Preserve EcoTour. This guide is unlike any other tour on Bocas del Toro! You go beyond dolphin-watching, jungle hiking, and snorkeling to experience nature. This tour provides you the chance to eat cocoa fruit straight from the pod, get up close and personal with poison dart frogs, caimans, and sea urchins, and learn about Bocas del Toro's rich socioeconomic and cultural heritage. During my stay in Bocas del Toro, I joined this guide. They picked me up at my hotel at exactly 10:00 am, by 10:30 am we were already at the Dolphin Bay for dolphin watching. By 11:00 am we started hiking. 1:30 pm was launch time and the guide provided us with locally made delicious food. I could remember I had Ceviche for lunch. It was truly delicious. At 2:00 pm we started Snorkeling and at 3:00 I was taken back to my hotel. It was truly a fun-filled day. so I'll advise you to join this tour guide.

5. The Enchanting Zapatilla Islands

Welcome to the Zapatilla Islands also called Cayos Zapatilla, an exquisite paradise tucked in the Bocas del Toro archipelago off Panama's Caribbean coast. If you're looking for beautiful beaches, crystal-clear oceans, and unrivaled natural beauty, look no further than this breathtaking location. Let's look at what makes the Zapatilla Islands a must-see destination and how to make the most of your vacation.

Getting There: Reaching the Zapatilla Islands is an adventure in itself, providing a peek at the breathtaking beauty that awaits you. The islands are part of the Bastimentos Island National Marine Park, which is located about 30 minutes by boat from the main island of Isla Colón. Visitors can easily organize boat trips or water taxi rides from Bocas Town or surrounding hotels to get to this isolated sanctuary.

As you glide across the turquoise waters of the Caribbean Sea, keep an eye out for dolphins playing in the waves and sea turtles gracefully swimming beneath the surface.

The journey to the Zapatilla Islands is more than just a method of transportation; it is an immersive experience that prepares the viewer for the delights that await.

Exploring the Zapatilla Islands: When you arrive in the Zapatilla Islands, you'll be met with a postcard-perfect landscape of powdery white sand beaches, swaying palm palms, and bright coral reefs alive with marine life. These uninhabited islands provide a pristine and undisturbed setting ideal for individuals seeking peace and natural beauty.

One of the delights of the Zapatilla Islands is the possibility of snorkeling and diving in the crystal-clear seas that surround them. Dive beneath the surface and see a kaleidoscope of colors as you encounter a variety of marine wildlife such as tropical fish, reef sharks, and vibrant coral formations. Whether you're an experienced diver or a first-time snorkeler, the underwater wonderland of the Zapatilla Islands will astound you.

For those who prefer to keep dry, the Zapatilla Islands' beaches provide plenty of chances for leisure and exploration. Take a stroll along the immaculate coastlines, bask in the sun on a private beach, or simply relax under a palm tree with a nice book. The islands' laid-back environment urges you to slow down, detach from the rush and bustle of daily life, and enjoy the serenity of your surroundings.

Unique Experiences: Making Memories on the Zapatilla Islands

In addition to snorkeling and beachcombing, the Zapatilla Islands provide a variety of unique experiences that are sure to leave a lasting impression.

- Take a guided nature trip through Bastimentos Island's beautiful rainforest, where you can see exotic creatures including sloths, monkeys, and tropical birds.

- Consider taking a kayaking tour across the islands to see secret coves, mangrove forests, and secluded lagoons. Paddle at your own pace, taking in the sights and sounds of nature, and feel exhilarated as you negotiate the Caribbean Sea's beautiful waters.
- As the day comes to a close, don't miss the chance to see a spectacular sunset over the Zapatilla Islands. Find a quiet location on the beach, watch the sky become pink, orange, and gold, and let the natural beauty steal your breath away.

The Zapatilla Islands are a true treasure of the Bocas del Toro archipelago, providing the ideal balance of natural beauty, adventure, and relaxation. Whether you're looking for an undersea adventure, a relaxing beach vacation, or an opportunity to reconnect with nature, the Zapatilla Islands have something for everyone. So pack your swimwear, take your camera, and prepare to witness the wonder of this tropical paradise firsthand.

6. Green Acres Chocolate Farms

Visit one of the most stunning nature preserves in Bocas Del Toro located on the shore of Dolphin Bay. This Nature preserve also offers a guided tour. This 2-hour tour brings you through lush tropical jungles, magnificent botanical gardens, and a massive Cacao Plantation. Animals abound on these 30 acres of heaven. Monkeys, toucans, sloths, poison dart frogs, tropical butterflies, and a variety of birds are frequently spotted. You can make reservations with the tour guide. Daily tours are usually available at 10 a.m. and 2 p.m.

Green Acres Chocolate Farms is more than simply a farm;

it's a chocolate enthusiast's dream. You'll be able to learn about the amazing process of manufacturing chocolate from bean to bar while immersed in the rainforest's sights, sounds, and fragrances. Whether you're a specialist or a casual enthusiast, a visit to Green Acres will tickle your taste buds and rekindle your love of chocolate.

Getting There: Green Acres Chocolate Farms is located on Isla Bastimentos, one of the principal islands in the Bocas del Toro archipelago, and is easily accessible by boat from Bocas Town. Simply take a water taxi or plan a tour with one of the local operators, and you'll be in Chocolate Paradise in no time. The journey itself is a spectacular excursion, with views of the crystal-clear waters and colorful marine life that surround the islands.

Exploring Green Acres

When you arrive at Green Acres Chocolate Farms, you will be greeted with great warmth from the staff and the delicious aroma of chocolate drifting through the air. Your guided tour will take you through the lush cocoa estate, where you'll learn about chocolate history, cacao tree cultivation, and traditional cacao bean harvesting and processing techniques.

One of the tour's attractions is the chance to engage in a hands-on chocolate manufacturing workshop.

You'll be able to roast, ground, and temper your chocolate with freshly picked cacao beans while being guided by experienced chocolatiers. Feel the smoothness of the melted chocolate as it runs between your fingers, and inhale the rich perfume as it fills the room. If you are part of a guided tour, you will typically be given delicious samples (including chocolate rum). The chocolate can also be purchased after the tour if you wish.

Unique Experiences

At Green Acres Chocolate Farms, the pleasure doesn't end with chocolate production. Visitors can also explore the neighboring jungle, which is home to tremendous biodiversity. Keep a watch out for unusual birds, butterflies, and other species as you walk around the woodland trails, and take in the spectacular views of the Caribbean Sea from the farm's hilltop vantage spots.

If you've been wishing to unwind and relax, Green Acres also has calm picnic spaces where you may have a leisurely lunch surrounded by natural beauty. You can enjoy the flavors of freshly prepared chocolate delights and tropical fruits while letting the stress of everyday life melt away in this gorgeous setting. So this must-see sight is a must-do when you visit Bocas del Toro..

7. Playa Bluff

Welcome to Playa Bluff, a hidden gem located on the gorgeous beaches of Bocas del Toro, Panama. Playa Bluff, with its wide coastline, beautiful sands, and untamed environment, is a haven for both beachgoers and adventurers. Let's go over everything you need to know about this lovely destination; Imagine yourself standing on the end of the planet, with nothing but the huge Caribbean Sea stretching out in front of you. That is the sensation you will feel at Playa Bluff. This vast beach spans for miles along the northeastern coast of Isla Colón, the main island of Bocas del Toro. As you step onto the powdered white sand, you'll be welcomed by the rhythmic crash of the waves and the salty breeze that caresses your skin. Playa Bluff is a location where time stands still, and every minute is filled with awe and peace.

Getting to Playa Bluff: While Playa Bluff may appear to be an isolated haven, it is rather accessible from the main town of Bocas del Toro. The most convenient method to get to Playa Bluff is to rent a bicycle or scooter and have a lovely ride along the coastline. The voyage lasts around 30 minutes and provides stunning views of the lush forests and crystal-clear waters. For those looking for a more adventurous path, you can hire a local guide to lead you on a hiking adventure into the forest. The walk to Playa Bluff goes through a lush forest, providing glimpses of unusual wildlife and panoramic views along the way.

Things to See and Do on Playa Bluff

Once you arrive at Playa Bluff, the opportunities for adventure are limitless. Here are some of the top things to see and do to maximize your experience:

- Surfing: Playa Bluff is known for its enormous waves, making it a destination for surfers from all over the world. Whether you're a seasoned surfer or a newbie catching your first wave, Playa Bluff's constant swell provides countless opportunities for exhilarating rides.

- Beachcombing: Take a stroll along the beach to find treasures washed up by the tide. From beautiful seashells to driftwood sculptures, you never know what treasures you'll find on Playa Bluff's immaculate sands.

- Sunbathing: Playa Bluff, with its huge expanse of golden sand and turquoise waters, is the ideal location to soak up the sun and work on your tan. Find a peaceful area, roll out your towel, and unwind to the relaxing sound of the waves.

- Wildlife Watching: Keep a look out for wildlife observations while you explore Playa Bluff. From cheerful dolphins frolicking in the surf to majestic frigatebirds soaring overhead, the beach is filled with intriguing species waiting to be discovered.

- Picnicking: Pack a picnic basket with your favorite snacks and refreshments, and enjoy a gorgeous lunch overlooking the Caribbean Sea's azure waves. There are numerous shady areas along the beach where you may set up a tent and enjoy a leisurely supper with loved ones.

- Photography: Using your camera or smartphone, capture the beauty of Playa Bluff to create lasting memories of your vacation. From breathtaking sunrise and sunset views to dramatic seascapes and craggy shorelines, every aspect provides a picture-perfect backdrop.

- Yoga and Meditation: Enjoy a yoga or meditation session on the beach while taking in the natural beauty of Playa Bluff. Feel the sand between your toes, the gentle air on your skin, and the soothing sound of the waves as you reconnect with yourself and the world around you. If you're new to Yoga, you can connect with the Roam Yoga and Wellness Center which is located on Isla Solarte, on the side facing Isla Bastimentos. It takes around 5 minutes or a little more to get there.

Whatever you decide to do with your stay at Playa Bluff, one thing is certain: you will leave with a heart full of memories and a soul refreshed by nature's beauty. So pack your swimwear, grab your sense of adventure, and set out for paradise at Playa Bluff in Bocas del Toro, Panama.

8. Polo Beach

Welcome to Polo Beach, a hidden gem located along Bocas del Toro's breathtaking coastline. This hidden sanctuary is ideal for anyone seeking peace, natural beauty, and pure seas. Polo Beach captivates visitors with its pristine white sands, crystal-clear blue waters, and lush tropical surroundings.

Tucked away on the secluded Bastimentos Island, this pristine sanctuary features breathtaking views of the Caribbean Sea and provides a tranquil getaway for both beachgoers and wildlife lovers. The beach is named after a famed "Polo" character who abandoned the spoils of civilization to live on this stretch of land for years. He, like many of the

Bastimentos' unusual indigenous frogs and other creatures, can still be seen on occasion in the area.

As you walk onto Polo Beach's smooth beaches, you'll be met by the steady cadence of waves lapping against the shore and the rustle of palm trees swinging in the wind. The beach spreads for miles, allowing plenty of room to spread out, relax, and soak up the sun in glorious tranquility.

How to get there

While Polo Beach is off the usual road, the drive to this gorgeous site is well worthwhile. Polo Beach is most commonly accessed via a short boat journey from Bocas del Toro's main town. Water taxis are widely accessible and can be booked through local tour operators or your lodging provider.

When you arrive at Bastimentos Island, you'll go on a picturesque hike through the jungle to Polo Beach. The hike lasts around 30 minutes and provides a sight of the island's diverse flora and fauna, including exotic species.

Things to See and Do

Polo Beach may be remote, but it provides plenty of opportunities for both action and relaxation. Here are some of the must-see places and activities to enjoy during your stay:

- Swimming & snorkeling: Dive into Polo Beach's crystal-clear waters to experience a vivid underwater world alive with colorful marine life. Grab your snorkeling gear and explore the coral reefs right offshore, where you'll see tropical fish, sea turtles, and other amazing animals.

- Beachcombing: Take a stroll along the shoreline in search of seashells, sand dollars, and other treasures washed up by the tide. Polo Beach, with its gorgeous sands and isolated position, provides the ideal setting for a relaxing beachcombing trip.

- Picnicking: Bring a nice picnic lunch and enjoy a gorgeous meal on the beach. Spread down a blanket, relax in the sun, and enjoy the flavors of fresh fruit, sandwiches, and local specialties while admiring the stunning seaside views.

- Sunset Watching: Watch the magic of a Bocas del Toro sunset from Polo Beach. As the sun sinks below the horizon, the sky explodes in a symphony of colors, casting a golden glow over the peaceful waters and producing a picture-perfect moment you'll never forget.

- Hiking: Put on your hiking boots and explore the picturesque trails that snake through the lush vegetation around Polo Beach. While exploring the island's unspoiled countryside, keep an eye out for animals such as monkeys, sloths, and tropical birds.

- Photography: Using your camera or smartphone, capture the beauty of Polo Beach to create lasting memories of your tropical vacation. From sweeping vistas to close-up shots of exotic flora and fauna, the beach provides limitless opportunities for spectacular photographs.

- Food and fruit drink: if you're lucky, you might spot "Polo," a man who has lived at Polo Beach for years and greets guests with open arms. He may provide you with wonderful cuisine for a small cost. The last time I visited Bocas del Toro, my companion and I left our hotel in Bocas Town, sailed to Isla Bastimentos, and then trekked to a beach called Polo Beach. While exploring the beach, we encountered Polo, an elderly and pleasant man.He took us to his cabin made of wood. Not quite long, We started licking our fingers, snacking on freshly caught fish he prepared, and sipping coconut water through a straw. It was a captivating experience for me.

Polo Beach is more than a location; it is an experience that will captivate you with its natural beauty and tranquility. Polo Beach provides something for everyone, whether you're looking for action, leisure, or just some peace in paradise.

So pack your luggage, put your troubles aside, and set out on a memorable vacation to this hidden treasure in Bocas del Toro.

9. The Plastic Bottle Village

Welcome to the Plastic Bottle Village, a unique site on Isla Colón in Bocas del Toro, Panama. Nestled in the lush tropical terrain, this eco-friendly oasis exemplifies human creativity and the force of sustainability. The plastic bottle hamlet includes a museum, a hotel, and a hostel. The Castle Inspiration is located in the Plastic Bottle Village. Robert Bezeau and his friends erected The Castle Inspiration between July 2016 and June 2018. It has four floors that are 14 meters (50 feet) high and built of 40,000 PET bottles. The Castle has four guest rooms on the first two stories, a dining area on the third, and a gathering level with a stunning view on the fourth. The primary goal is to excite

and educate tourists, as well as to raise awareness about the invasion of single-use PET plastic bottles into our oceans. Prepare to be astounded as you begin on a quest to discover this incredible village constructed solely of plastic bottles.

Getting There

Getting to Plastic Bottle Village is an adventure in itself. The town, located just a short distance from Bocas Town on Isla Colón, is easily accessible by taxi, bicycle, or foot. As you go through the meandering jungle roads, you'll catch glimpses of the blue Caribbean Sea through the trees, generating excitement for the treasures that await you.

When you arrive in the Plastic Bottle Village, you'll be greeted with warm smiles and a unique sense of camaraderie. The town is open to visitors year-round and offers guided tours that explain the ingenious construction processes utilized to create this ecological beauty.

Exploring the Plastic Bottle Village

Step inside the Plastic Bottle Village and prepare to be transported to a world where waste is turned into artwork. Everywhere you look, there are bright walls, elaborate sculptures, and fanciful buildings made from thousands of recycled plastic bottles. It's a breathtaking sight that demonstrates the human spirit's ingenuity and resourcefulness.

As you go around the hamlet, take in the delicate features of each masterpiece. From towering sculptures to small cottages, each construction conveys a message about sustainability and environmental responsibility. Remember to bring your camera so you may capture the charm of this one-of-a-kind destination and share it with the world.

Unique Things to See and Do

To make the most of your visit to the Plastic Bottle Village, there are numerous interesting things to see and do, including:

- Take a guided tour: Join a guided tour given by educated residents who will explain the history and vision of Plastic Bottle Village. Learn about the construction process, . the village's objective to promote sustainability and the creative ways discarded materials are reused.

- Attend a class: Get hands-on experience and release your creativity by taking part in a class guided by local artists and craftspeople. Learn how to make your eco-friendly constructions out of recycled materials and leave with a one-of-a-kind souvenir to remember your stay.

- Relax in Nature: Take a minute to relax and reconnect with nature in the peaceful settings of the Plastic Bottle Village. Take a stroll through the jungle paths, listening to the relaxing sounds of songbirds and admiring the spectacular vistas of the surrounding area.

- Support Local Artisans: Explore the village's onsite gallery and shop, where you'll find a wide range of handcrafted items created by local craftsmen. From jewelry and textiles to home decor and artwork, there is something for everyone to find and treasure.

Special Places to Visit in the Plastic Bottle Village
- The Bottle House: Enter this fanciful edifice built entirely of plastic bottles to marvel at its creative design. Homes available here are also built with plastic bottles.
- The Eco-Cathedral: Explore this gorgeous cathedral, which features brilliant mosaics and stained glass windows made from recyclable materials.
- The Bottle Garden: Walk through lush gardens full of exotic plants and flowers, all growing in soil enhanced with compost generated from recycled organic waste.
- The Eco-Laboratory: Explore the village's current research and development programs centered on sustainability and environmental conservation.
- Museum: This enchanting place has a museum that has diverse beautiful paintings.

As you leave the Plastic Bottle Village, take a minute to think about the profound impact of your visit. You have seen personally the transforming power of creativity, innovation, and sustainability. Carry these lessons with you as you continue your trip, inspired to make a positive change in the world and preserve the environment for future generations.

10. Rio San San

Welcome to Rio San San, a hidden gem deep in Panama's gorgeous rainforest. Rio San San, with its pure river, deep jungle environs, and numerous wildlife, provides an immersive natural experience that will leave you in amazement.

Getting There: To get to Rio San San, start your adventure in the colorful town of Bocas del Toro. From there, you can take a picturesque boat trip along the coast, passing by mangrove forests and idyllic islands. As you cruise around the peaceful seas, keep a lookout for dolphins frolicking in the surf.

After around 45 minutes, you'll reach the mouth of Rio San San, where the river meets the sea. From here, you can continue your adventure upstream by boat or kayak, taking in the natural splendor around you.

Exploring Rio San San

When you arrive in Rio San San, you'll be met with the  sights and sounds of the jungle. Towering trees form a canopy overhead, with exotic birds flitting among the branches and monkeys chattering in the background. It is an enjoyable place for those who love nature and adventure.

Unique Things to Do and See
- River Safari: Take an exciting river safari along Rio San San, where you'll negotiate twisting waterways and see a variety of species. Keep your camera handy

as you observe colorful birds, languid sloths, and elusive caimans hiding in the shallows.

- Waterfall Hike: Put on your hiking boots and head into the woods to find hidden waterfalls nestled away in remote areas of Rio San San. Take a soothing dip in the crystal-clear pools beneath the flowing waters, surrounded by natural sights and sounds.

- Cacao Plantation Tour: A guided tour of a local cacao plantation will provide insight into Panama's rich history of chocolate manufacture. Learn about the traditional methods for cultivating and harvesting cacao beans, and try freshly produced chocolate delights right from the source.

- Watching Manatees Up Close: Take a guided tour conducted by professional naturalists from AAMVECONA to learn about these gentle giants' behavior, habitat, and conservation efforts. AAMVECONA, an abbreviation for Asociación Amigos de la Naturaleza y Vida Silvestre en Costa y Oro Norte de Panamá, is a conservation organization that works to safeguard the local ecosystem and animals, especially the endangered

West Indian manatee. To reach AAMVECONA, take a bus from Bocas town, passing through Las Tablas and Changuinola. This method is inexpensive, costing approximately $11-$14, and takes 2 hours and 41 minutes. If you're good in Spanish you can make your visit more memorable. Enter the AAMVECONA office upstairs and request a boat to the platform in Spanish from one of the workers of the tour guide. He will notify the boat captain and charge you $70/boat plus $5/person, with a maximum of 10 persons per boat for the guide. You must send them (AAMVECONA) an email in advance of your planned visit. After all necessary payments have been made, you will be given a life jacket and transported by boat down Rio San San to the San San Pond Sak HUMEDAL (wetlands area). You'll observe turtles and a large number of manatees looking for their favorite aquatic plants. When you get to the platform, you'll notice manatees feeding. Your guide will allow you to feed the manatees with hanging bananas.

- Sunset Kayaking: Wrap up your day in Rio San San with a leisurely kayak cruise along the river as the sun sets over the horizon. Paddle softly through mangrove-lined waterways, taking in the golden glow of the fading light and the serenity of your surroundings.

Unique Places to Visit

- Isla Pájaros, sometimes known as "Bird Island," is a small island refuge that hosts thousands of nesting birds such as frigatebirds, pelicans, and herons. Take a guided boat cruise to see birds in flight and take beautiful shots of the avian inhabitants.

- Boca del Drago: Discover the pristine beaches and coral reefs of Boca del Drago, a charming coastal community near the mouth of Rio San San. Relax on the smooth sands, snorkel among the colorful marine life, and eat freshly caught seafood at one of the local eateries.

- Starfish Beach: Explore the beauty of Starfish Beach, where shallow turquoise waters and pure white beaches provide the ideal environment for a day of leisure. Look for beautiful starfish spread around the seashore, or take a walk down the beach to collect seashells and enjoy the sun.

In Rio San San, every turn exposes a new wonder waiting to be explored. Whether you're going on a jungle adventure, exploring hidden waterfalls, or simply admiring the natural beauty, Rio San San guarantees a memorable experience that will leave you feeling renewed and inspired. So come, and immerse yourself in the magic of this tropical paradise; adventure awaits!

11. Boca del Drago

Welcome to Boca del Drago, a hidden gem located on the northern edge of Isla Colón in Bocas del Toro, Panama. This picturesque beach spot provides guests with a peaceful respite from the stresses of everyday life, complete with crystal-clear waters and powdered white sands.

Boca del Drago is known for its pure beauty and calm setting. As you walk onto the beaches of this hidden paradise, you'll be welcomed by breathtaking vistas of the Caribbean Sea stretching out before you.

The beach itself is surrounded by lush green palm trees that wave softly in the ocean wind, providing the ideal setting for a day of relaxation and refreshment.

How to Get There

Getting to Boca del Drago is simple, whether you stay in Bocas Town or on one of the adjacent islands. From Bocas Town, you can take a water taxi or book a guided tour to Isla Colón. Once on the island, Boca del Drago is only a short drive or bike ride away. If you're feeling daring, you may even rent a kayak and paddle your way to this remote beach paradise.

Things to See and Do

When you arrive in Boca del Drago, you will discover plenty of activities to keep you busy. Here are some must-see places and memorable experiences to include on your itinerary:

- Starfish Beach, also known as Playa Estrella, is a short walk from Boca del Drago and is named after the many starfish that live in its shallow waters. Spend the day snorkeling among beautiful coral reefs, relaxing on the smooth sand, or admiring the natural beauty that surrounds you.
- Red Frog Beach: For those seeking excitement, a trip to Red Frog Beach is essential. This magnificent beach, located just a short boat trip from Boca del Drago, offers a variety of activities such as surfing,

zip-lining, and trekking along lush rainforest trails. Keep an eye out for the renowned red poison dart frogs that gave the beach its name.

- Punta Hospital: To experience local culture and history, head to Punta Hospital, a historic monument in Boca del Drago. You can visit the remnants of a historic hospital from the early twentieth century, which provide an intriguing view of the island's history.

- Bird Watching: Boca del Drago is also a birdwatcher's paradise, with a variety of tropical bird species living there. Grab your binoculars and look for colorful parrots, toucans, and hummingbirds as you explore the surrounding jungle.

Boca del Drago is a true paradise waiting to be discovered, boasting pristine beaches, crystal-clear waters, and an abundance of natural beauty. Whether you choose action or relaxation, this charming destination has something for everyone. So pack your sunscreen, take your camera, and prepare to embark on the perfect tropical getaway in Boca del Drago, Panama.

Hidden Gems

Welcome to Bocas del Toro, where hidden treasures and secret surprises await discovery. While the main attractions are stunning in their beauty and popularity, it is the off-the-beaten-path encounters that truly capture the soul of this enchanting location. Join us as we reveal some of Bocas del Toro's best-kept secrets, handpicked by locals who know how to navigate this tropical paradise.

1. The Mangrove Forests on Isla Bastimentos

The beautiful mangrove woodlands, hidden away on the fringes of Isla Bastimentos, await exploration. Take a guided kayak or boat excursion along winding rivers flanked by towering mangrove trees, where the peaceful sounds of nature will serenade you as you paddle. Keep a watch out for unique species, such as sloths relaxing in the treetops and colorful birds darting through the canopy. For the daring, explore a midnight bioluminescent cruise, when the waters come alive with shimmering lights, producing a magnificent display unlike anything you've seen before.

Getting there: To get to Isla Bastimentos, take a short water taxi ride from Bocas Town to its main port. From there, you may schedule a guided trip to the mangrove woods with one of the local tour providers.

2. The Caves of Isla Colón

Under the surface of Isla Colón, there is a hidden world of caves and caverns waiting to be discovered. Set off on a fascinating spelunking expedition via tiny corridors and underground chambers, lighted by the soothing glow of your headlight. Admire old rock formations etched by millennia of natural forces, and listen for the echoes of your footsteps as you journey deeper into the earth's core. Consider attending a guided cave diving excursion to explore subterranean caves filled with aquatic life.

One of these caves is **La Gruta**. For an adventure unlike any other, head deep into the jungle to find La Gruta, a subterranean cave system cloaked in mystery and intrigue. To reach La Gruta, you must hike through lush rainforest trails and ford creeks. That's why guided tours are important. They'll help you easily get to these hidden gems. Once inside, you'll be stunned by the cave's unearthly beauty, complete with beautiful rock formations and an ethereal glow. Take a guided tour to explore the labyrinthine tunnels and learn about the cave's geological history, or simply wander at your leisure and absorb the sense of wonder that surrounds you. Just make sure you have strong shoes and a sense of adventure, as exploring the cave can be difficult but rewarding.

Getting there: The Isla Colón caverns are accessible by boat or kayak from Bocas Town. Once on the island, you can hire a local guide to take you on a cave exploration excursion.

3. The Hidden Beaches of Isla Carenero

Escape the throng and find your slice of paradise on Isla Carenero's isolated beaches. These hidden gems, surrounded by lush palm palms and lapped by crystal-clear seas, make the ideal environment for a day of rest and regeneration. Pack a picnic lunch and spend the day relaxing on exquisite white sands, snorkeling in vibrant coral reefs, or simply basking in the sun with a good book in hand. For those wanting adventure, rent a stand-up paddleboard and explore the coastline at your leisure, discovering hidden coves and secret beaches along the way.

Getting there: Isla Carenero is simply a short water taxi journey from Bocas Town. When you get on the island, you may easily explore the secret beaches on foot or rent a bicycle from one of the local rental shops.

4. Isla San Cristobal

Immerse yourself in the rich cultural history of Isla San Cristobal's indigenous Ngöbe-Buglé people. Discover traditional villages tucked in beautiful jungles, where you may learn about centuries-old customs and traditions passed down through generations. Participate in a traditional dance celebration, experience authentic cuisine produced with locally sourced ingredients, and shop for handmade goods and souvenirs created by local craftsmen. Consider spending overnight in a community-run eco-lodge, where you can interact with nature and learn about sustainable living techniques directly from the indigenous residents.

Getting there: The island of San Cristobal is accessible by boat from Bocas Town. Once you arrive on the island, you can schedule a guided cultural tour with one of the local community leaders.

5. Finca Los Monos Botanical Garden

To experience rural life in Bocas del Toro, head inland to Finca Los Monos, a quaint family-owned farm located in the center of the island. Getting to Finca Los Monos is an experience in itself, as you wind your way through thick jungle trails and across rustic wooden bridges, taking in the island's natural splendor along the way.

When you arrive at the farm, you will be met by friendly locals who want to share their way of life with you. A guided tour of the farm allows you to learn about sustainable agriculture practices and eat freshly gathered fruits directly from the tree. You can also join in hands-on activities like coffee roasting, chocolate making, and traditional cooking workshops to learn about Bocas del Toro's rich cultural legacy.

6. Nivida Bat Caves

Nivida, one of Bastimentos' most remarkable natural wonders, is a large cave filled with nectar bats and an underground lake. Nivida Bat Cave is a hidden gem within the Bastimentos Island National Marine Park. Since its discovery in the early 2000s, the cave has been run by a local family, with one of the two brothers guiding visitors

through. The cave contains hundreds of nectar bats, most of which live around the entrance. The cave grows tighter as you go deeper. If you don't want to get wet or dislike small or tight places, stay at the entrance. This is one of the most interesting activities available in Bocas del Toro and one of my personal favorites.

To explore the cave, first go to Bocas del Toro from Panama's main town. Then, plan a bat cave tour. I'll strongly advise you to take a local guide, so you don't miss your way.

You can book a tour from Old Bank to the cave. It costs $45 per person. The excursion includes a 25-minute boat ride from the Old Bank to the channel entrance. You will then skim over mangroves and lush flora. From the dock, it's a half-hour climb to the cave. Wear sturdy shoes or boots; you'll be given headlights at the cave entrance.

However, If you are more daring and adventurous you can get to Nivida without any guide. To do this first arrive at Isla Colon. When you arrive on the island, wander along the main strip of Bocas Town and look for signs providing tours of the bat cave. If you're traveling with a group of four or more people, you can also book a water taxi. The 20-minute speedboat or water taxi ride from town will take you to Bahia Honda, where you will journey through the mangroves for 15 minutes before arriving at the private property; Parque Nacional Isla Bastimentos. Keep an eye out for dolphins and sloths. I saw some of each. Pay a minimal entrance fee that includes your guide, a headlamp, and water shoes. Prepare to hike. The journey through the jungle to the cave takes 10-20 minutes, depending on your stops along the route.

Once at the entrance, turn on your headlamp and prepare to enter. The majority of bats are found at the cave's entrance. Looking up, you'll notice that most of them are asleep, but a few are soaring around the cave. It's awesome to see them active. I must warn you to avoid looking up with your lips open. You don't want anything to fall in your mouth. Also, when shooting images with your headlight, avoid looking directly at the camera, to prevent the image from being too bright. Look to the side and ensure that the person taking your shot does not shine their light straight at you.

7. Enchanting Waterfalls on Bastimentos Island

Hidden deep within the heart of Bastimentos Island, a series of magnificent waterfalls await discovery. To begin this journey, take a water taxi from Bocas Town to Bastimentos and request that your captain drop you off near the jungle trail's entrance. From there, it's a magnificent journey through dense jungle, crossing streams and navigating steep terrain until you reach the flowing waters of the waterfalls.

As you approach the falls, you'll hear rushing water and see green pools nestled among moss-covered rocks. Take a soothing dip in the calm waters, swim among the waterfalls, and enjoy the natural beauty that surrounds you. For the more daring, there are prospects for cliff jumping and rock scrambling, but act with caution and always respect natural forces.

The journey from Nivida Bat Cave ends at a little waterfall with a deep pool for swimming. At this point, there are currently no more bats. You can relax or swim.

From hidden caves to isolated beaches, Bocas del Toro is overflowing with off-the-beaten-path experiences waiting to be explored. Whether you're an adventurer, nature lover, or culture buff, these hidden gems provide a glimpse into the actual soul of this tropical paradise. So, get off the beaten route and discover the secrets of Bocas del Toro.

CHAPTER FOUR

Outdoor Activities & Cultural Experiences

Snorkeling and Diving in Bocas del Toro

Are you ready to explore the fascinating underwater world of Bocas del Toro? From bright coral reefs to unique marine life, the archipelago provides some of the best snorkeling and diving opportunities in the Caribbean.

Whether you're an experienced diver or a first-time snorkeler, there's something for everyone beneath the crystal-clear waters of Bocas del Toro.

Snorkeling

Snorkeling is an excellent opportunity to get up close and personal with Bocas del Toro's vibrant marine life without requiring professional training or equipment. Simply put on your mask, snorkel, and fins, and prepare to be surprised by the beauty that exists beneath the surface.

Where To Snorkel:

- Starfish Beach: A short boat journey from Isla Colón, Starfish Beach is well-known for its shallow, tranquil waters and richness of marine life. While snorkeling around the shoreline, keep a lookout for starfish, colorful fish, and the occasional marine turtle.
- Coral Gardens: Located near Bastimentos Island, Coral Gardens is a snorkeler's dream. Swim among bright coral formations rich with tropical fish, and keep an eye out for moray eels, rays, and nurse sharks.

Local Guides: For an amazing snorkeling experience, arrange a guided excursion with one of Bocas del Toro's reputed tour operators. Companies such as Bocas Water Sports and Bocas Dive Center provide half-day and full-day snorkeling tours led by knowledgeable guides who know the finest places to visit. The Bocas dive center is located at Isla Colon, C. 4ta, Bocas del Toro, Panama. You can call them for more information by dialing +507 6348-9597.

Cost and Gear Rental: Most snorkeling tours in Bocas del Toro include equipment rental as part of the package. Prices vary based on the length of the tour and the operator but expect to pay between $25 and $50 per person for a half-day trip. If you want to snorkel on your own, you may rent snorkeling equipment from shops and rental companies in Bocas Town for about $10 to $20 per day.

Diving

For those looking for a more immersive underwater experience, diving in Bocas del Toro offers excitement and discovery at every turn. Divers of all skill levels will find plenty of excitement among the numerous dive locations, which range from shallow reefs to deep wrecks.

Where to dive: The Playground, located off the shore of Bastimentos Island, is a renowned diving location recognized for its diverse marine life and spectacular coral reefs. Look for schools of colorful fish, reef sharks, and octopuses as you explore the underwater playground.

- Hospital Point: Located near Isla Carenero, Hospital Point allows divers to see larger marine species such as barracudas, stingrays, and the odd hammerhead shark. The setting includes undulating coral cliffs and rocky outcrops alive with life.

Local Guides: Consider diving with a professional dive operator in Bocas del Toro for a safe and enjoyable experience. Companies such as La Buga Dive & Surf and Pirate Island Divers provide guided dive trips to the region's most prominent dive spots, led by qualified instructors who promote safety and conservation. You can visit the La Buga Dive & Surf website at https://labugapanama.com/ for more information.

Cost and Gear Rental: The cost of diving at Bocas del Toro varies based on the number of dives, equipment rental, and certification level. A single tank dive is normally priced between $50 and $80, with savings available for multiple dives or diving packages. Equipment rental, which includes tanks, regulators, and wetsuits, is typically included in the dive price, although you can hire gear separately if necessary. Whether you prefer to snorkel among the shallow reefs or dive deep into the Caribbean Sea, discovering Bocas del Toro's underwater delights is an unforgettable experience. So grab your mask and fins, and prepare to dive into adventure in this tropical paradise.

Insider tip: for a memorable diving experience, try night diving. It's a fun-filled experience.

Surfing in Bocas del Toro

Are you ready to catch some waves in one of the world's most gorgeous surf destinations? Welcome to Bocas del Toro, where turquoise waters and regular swells make it a surfer's dream. Whether you're a seasoned pro or a newbie eager to hang ten for the first time, Bocas del Toro provides an incredible surfing experience that will have you wanting more.

Bocas del Toro has a wide variety of surf breaks ideal for surfers of all levels. There is something for everyone here, from relaxing beach breaks to difficult reef breaks. The archipelago's unique terrain and location in the Caribbean

Sea provide perfect surfing conditions all year, with the best waves falling between December and April.

Where To Surf

Wizard Beach, on Isla Bastimentos, is one of Bocas del Toro's most popular surf places. This remote beach has regular waves and breathtaking scenery, making it a favorite

 among surfers seeking peace and huge rides. For surfers seeking a more challenging experience, Paunch Beach and Dumpers are well-known for their powerful reef breakers and hollow barrels.

If you're new to surfing or want to improve your skills, there are several surf schools and instructors in Bocas del Toro that offer lessons and guided tours. Bocas Surf School, located on Isla Colón, is a highly recommended choice. Bocas Surf School, run by experienced local surfers, provides personalized instruction based on your skill level, providing a safe and pleasurable learning experience in the ocean.

Rental Gear

Don't worry about dragging your surfboard halfway around the world; Bocas del Toro offers dozens of rental shops where you may prepare for your surfing experience. Island Traders Surf Shop, located in the heart of Bocas Town, has a large assortment of surfboards, ranging from beginner-friendly softtops to high-performance shortboards. You can also hire other necessary equipment, such as leashes, wax, and rash guards, to ensure a comfortable and fun surf session.

Costs: The cost of renting surf gear in Bocas del Toro varies according to the length of the rental and the type of equipment used. Surfboard rentals typically cost between $20 and $30 per day, with reductions available for extended rental periods. Lessons and guiding services cost $50 to $100 per session, depending on the duration and instructor's ability.

Safety Tip: Surfing in Bocas del Toro is an exciting activity, but it is critical to prioritize safety and respect for the ocean. Before going out, verify the surf conditions and weather prediction, and always surf within your skill level. Be alert of your surroundings and keep an eye out for other surfers, swimmers, and marine creatures in the water. Also, be aware of local surf etiquette and show respect for the local population and environment.

Surfing at Bocas del Toro provides an unrivaled blend of world-class waves, breathtaking landscapes, and a relaxed island ambiance. Whether you're a newbie wanting to catch your first wave or an experienced pro looking for new challenges, Bocas del Toro has something for everyone. So take your board, wax it, and prepare to ride the waves in paradise.

Wildlife Watching

Welcome to the wild side of Bocas del Toro, where lush rainforests, pristine beaches, and crystal-clear waters create the ideal setting for amazing wildlife encounters. Whether you're a nature lover, an animal lover, or simply looking for a deeper connection with the natural world, Bocas del Toro has a plethora of wildlife-watching options that will leave

you blown away. Bocas del Toro has a diversified ecosystem with unique species both on land and in water. The archipelago is home to a diverse range of animals, including exotic birds, playful dolphins, elusive sloths, and brilliant reef fish. Whether you're exploring the deep rainforest of Isla Bastimentos or snorkeling in the beautiful coral gardens of Cayos Zapatilla, there will be plenty of opportunities to watch and connect with the locals.

Where to go for wildlife watching

- Isla Bastimentos National Marine Park: This protected region is a wildlife hotspot, with dense mangrove forests, rich tropical vegetation, and beautiful beaches offering ideal habitat for a diverse range of species. Take a guided boat tour through the park's twisting canals to see sloths lazing in the trees, scarlet poison dart frogs hopping along the forest floor, and colorful toucans flying through the canopy. Eco Bocas Tours such as Bastimentos Alive provides informative and environmentally friendly guided tours to Isla Bastimentos National Marine Park, led by skilled local guides who are dedicated to conservation and wildlife preservation. They provide customized excursions based on your preferences and timetable, ensuring an amazing experience for nature enthusiasts of all ages.

- Dolphin Bay, a quiet cove just a short boat ride from Bocas Town, is home to pods of bottlenose dolphins that feed, play, and socialize. Join a guided dolphin-watching expedition to see these clever marine creatures in their natural habitat, jumping gracefully out of the water and doing jaw-dropping acrobatic performances. I recommend the Bocas Sailing tour guide. They provide small-group dolphin-watching cruises led by expert captains who know the finest places to see dolphins in Dolphin Bay. Their environmentally conscientious approach guarantees that the animals are disturbed as little as possible, allowing you to watch them in their natural habitat without causing harm.

- Cayo Coral Reef: Put on your snorkel gear and dive into the crystal-clear waters of Cayo Coral Reef, a natural marine sanctuary rich with vibrant coral formations, tropical fish, and other sea life. Swim with colorful parrot fish, agile eagle rays, and elusive sea turtles as you explore Bocas del Toro's underwater wonderland.

Rental Gears: Aqua Lounge Dive Shop, located on Isla Carenero, provides snorkel gear rentals at reasonable prices. Whether you need a mask, fins, snorkel, or a whole set of equipment, their helpful team will make sure you have everything you need for a memorable snorkeling trip.

Snorkel gear rentals at Aqua Lounge Dive Shop begin at $10 per day for a basic set, with extra equipment available for an additional fee.

Costs of Wildlife Watching Activities: Guided excursions at Isla Bastimentos National Marine Park normally cost $30 to $50 per person, depending on the length and scope of the tour. Dolphin-watching tours in Dolphin Bay are normally priced between $25 and $40 per person, with discounts available for children and group reservations.

From the deep jungles of Isla Bastimentos to the crystal-clear waters of Dolphin Bay and Cayo Coral Reef, Bocas del Toro has countless possibilities for animal viewing that will leave you feeling inspired, amazed, and connected to the natural world. So grab your binoculars, camera, and spirit of adventure, and set off on a tour into the heart of paradise, where every encounter with nature is a memory to treasure forever.

Immerse Yourself in the Cultural Tapestry of Bocas del Toro

In Bocas del Toro, a vibrant tapestry of indigenous culture weaves across the lush landscapes and dazzling waterways of this tropical haven. Don't pass up the opportunity to engage with the intriguing indigenous cultures that live in Bocas del Toro. These towns, with their rich traditions and strong connection to the land and water, provide a look into a way of life that is both beautiful and ancient.

Discovering Indigenous Communities

Several indigenous populations have lived in Bocas del Toro for millennia, nestled among the lush woods and gorgeous coasts. The Ngäbe-Buglé and Naso (Teribe) are the two largest indigenous groups in the area, each with their language, rituals, and traditions. These villages have managed to preserve their way of life in the face of modernity, making them unique repositories of cultural history.

Getting there: Travelers can discover the rich cultural history of Bocas del Toro's indigenous tribes through guided excursions given by local operators or by arranging visits directly with community leaders. Many indigenous villages are accessible via boat or trekking paths, allowing visitors to immerse themselves in the region's natural splendor while traveling to these distant settlements.

Things to See and Do: When you arrive in an Indigenous village, you will be met with friendly faces and a plethora of cultural activities to discover. Here are a few examples of what you can see and do:

- Traditional Ceremonies and Festivals: Participating in traditional rites and festivals allows you to see the vibrant nature of Indigenous culture firsthand. These festivities, which include vivid dances and old rituals, provide an intriguing peek into indigenous tribes' spiritual beliefs and customs.
- Artisan Workshops: Visit local craftsmen's workshops to see how they make traditional crafts including handwoven textiles, elaborate beading, and wooden carvings. You can also try your hand at making your keepsake with the help of experienced artists.
- Cultural demonstrations: Learn about traditional practices like hunting, fishing, and agriculture

through participatory demonstrations presented by residents. Learn about indigenous tribes' sustainable lifestyles and their strong regard for nature.

- Community homestays: Staying in a community-run homestay allows you to become immersed in the daily lives of indigenous cultures. Share meals with your hosts, join in daily activities, and have meaningful discussions about their culture and way of life.

- Natural Walks and Eco-Tours: Guided nature hikes and eco-tours provide opportunities to explore the unspoiled wilderness around Indigenous villages. Knowledgeable local guides will teach you about the rainforest's medicinal plants, fauna, and ecological value.

Valuable Tips

- Respect local customs: When visiting indigenous villages, it is critical to honor their customs, traditions, and way of life. Seek permission before photographing, adhere to any cultural protocols, and avoid trespassing on sacred sites.

- Support Sustainable tourism: Choose tour operators and accommodations that prioritize sustainable tourism practices and contribute to local communities. Your travel choices can help to preserve indigenous cultures and save natural resources.

- Learn Basic Phrases: While many community members know Spanish, learning a few words or phrases in the local indigenous language can show respect and gratitude for their heritage. Simple pleasantries like "Buenos días" (good morning) or "gracias" (thank you) help build meaningful friendships.

Taking a cultural tour through Bocas del Toro's indigenous communities provides an incredible opportunity to engage with the rich tapestry of human experience. Travelers can get a deeper awareness of the interconnection of all living beings and the need to maintain cultural diversity for future generations by immersing themselves in these ancient nations' traditions, rituals, and lifestyles. So, bundle your curiosity and embark on a transforming journey into the heart of Bocas del Toro's indigenous culture.

Festivals of Bocas del Toro

Welcome to Bocas del Toro, where life revolves around vivid festivals and cultural celebrations. The Bocas del Toro festivals, which range from traditional rites to boisterous street celebrations, provide tourists with a one-of-a-kind opportunity to immerse themselves in Panamanian culture. Prepare to dance, feast, and revel like a local as we visit some of the most memorable festivals and events that this magical archipelago offers.

1. Carnival at Bocas del Toro: Carnival, Bocas del Toro's largest and most anticipated annual event, kicks off the festivities. Carnival, which takes place yearly in the weeks preceding Lent (March 1st-4th), is typically a raucous festival of music, dance, and revelry that brings the entire community together in a frenzy of color and excitement.

- Where: The biggest Carnival celebrations take place in Bocas Town on Isla Colón, where street parades, live music performances, and costume contests turn the town into a pulsating carnival capital.
- Getting There: To join in the Carnival fun, head to Bocas Town on Isla Colón. Whether you stay on the main island or one of the smaller surrounding

islands, water taxis, and ferries make it easy to get to the festivities.

- What to Expect: During Carnival, the streets of Bocas Town become a kaleidoscope of colors, with both locals and visitors dressed in vivid costumes and masks. Join the stream of dancers as they move through the streets to the irresistible rhythms of salsa, reggaeton, and calypso. Enjoy authentic Panamanian street cuisine and cool drinks from sellers lining the streets, and don't miss the Carnival Queen's coronation.

2. The Sea Fair (La Feria del Mar): La Feria del Mar, or Sea Fair, is a must-see for those interested in Bocas del Toro's marine legacy. This colorful celebration, held every September, commemorates the archipelago's relationship to the sea with a broad program of nautical-themed activities and entertainment.

- Where: La Feria del Mar is held in Bocas Town, Isla Colón, with the shoreline turned into a busy hive of nautical festivities.
- Getting There: To get to Bocas Town for La Feria del Mar, simply take a water taxi or ferry from your

hotel or neighboring island. The event is easily accessible from all around the archipelago.

- What to Expect: At La Feria del Mar, tourists may watch colorful sailboat regattas, traditional fishing competitions, and thrilling water sports exhibitions. The waterfront food stalls serve freshly caught seafood delights made by local chefs, while the lively market sells artisanal crafts and souvenirs. Don't miss live performances by local musicians and dance troupes, who will keep the party going well into the night.

3. Festival del Cristo Negro (Black Christ Festival): The Festival del Cristo Negro, a religious pilgrimage and celebration celebrated annually in October in the mainland village of Portobelo, offers an opportunity to explore the junction of faith and culture.

- Where: The Festival del Cristo Negro is held at Portobelo, a historic port town on Panama's mainland coast, about two hours from Bocas del Toro.

- Getting There: While Portobelo is located on the mainland, travelers from Bocas del Toro can easily access the town via water taxis, buses, or rental cars.

Alternatively, visitors seeking a hassle-free vacation can take advantage of guided tours to Portobelo.

- What to Expect: The Festival del Cristo Negro revolves around the veneration of the Black Christ, a sacred religious figure located in the medieval Church of San Felipe. Join pilgrims from Panama and beyond as they march through Portobelo's streets, bearing statues of the Black Christ and chanting devotional hymns. Witness the strong sense of faith and reverence in the air as pilgrims pay tribute to their beloved patron saint. Following the religious services, the town comes alive with traditional music, dance, and street food, resulting in a joyous scene that honors both spirituality and community.

4. Bocas Chocolate Fair: Indulge your sweet craving and learn about chocolate's rich history at the Bocas Showcolate Fair, an annual celebration of cacao and culture held on October 1st. It's all about the Bocas del Toro chocolate and cocoa. It is an educational event focused on the protection of rainforests, cocoa farmers, and cultural legacy. Local and international chocolate manufacturers compete in a chocolate confection contest. Every guest gets to test each submission. There are cacao-related seminars, exhibitions, workshops, chocolate-themed beverages, and live music. Money is raised to help The Darklands Foundation's (the fair's organizer) efforts to develop industrial prospects for Ngäbe-Buglé Indigenous people (especially women). This event is normally held at the LostBoys Blues Bar, commonly referred to as Casa Chocolate, situated in PirateArts.

5. Bocas Arts and Music Festival: This is a celebration of creativity. Experience Bocas del Toro's thriving arts scene at the annual Bocas Arts and Music Festival, which displays the skills of local artists, musicians, and performers from all around the region.

- Where: The Bocas Arts and Music Festival is held in several venues around Bocas del Toro, including Bocas Town on Isla Colón and nearby islands Bastimentos and Carenero.

- Getting There: To attend the Bocas Arts and Music Festival, take a water taxi or shuttle to Bocas Town or any of the other participating venues. The festival organizers arrange transportation for attendees staying on several islands, ensuring easy access to all festival events.

- What to Expect: The Bocas Arts and Music Festival offers a diverse program of live music concerts, art exhibitions, film screenings, and cultural seminars. Discover local artists' diverse talents as they display paintings, sculptures, and handicrafts inspired by the natural beauty and cultural legacy of Bocas del Toro. Dance the night away to the sounds of reggae, salsa, and calypso music, performed by great musicians from Panama and beyond. The Bocas Arts and Music Festival is a lively celebration of creativity and community spirit, with food vendors selling tasty snacks and refreshments, as well as engaging activities for children and families.

Bocas del Toro provides tourists with a one-of-a-kind opportunity to immerse themselves in Panama's vibrant culture and traditions through a variety of festivals and events honoring everything from chocolate to music. Whether you're dancing in the streets during Carnival, indulging in chocolate delicacies at the Chocolate Fair, or discovering the local art scene during the Bocas Arts and Music Festival, these cultural events will leave you with lifelong memories. So come celebrate and experience the enchantment of Bocas del Toro's festivals and events.

Discovering the Art and Craft Traditions

Welcome to Bocas del Toro, where Caribbean rhythms blend with a vibrant tapestry of local culture. Beyond the

sun-kissed beaches and lush rainforests, you'll uncover a rich heritage of art and craft traditions that capture the essence of this lovely archipelago.

Art of Bocas del Toro: Art is woven into the fabric of everyday life in Bocas del Toro, from vibrant paintings on the streets of Isla Colón to elaborately woven textiles created by Indigenous groups. Immerse yourself in the local art scene and feel the creative energy that characterizes this tropical paradise.

- Murals & Street Art: A stroll through the streets of Bocas Town will reveal a kaleidoscope of colors splattered on building facades and alleyways. Local artists use the town's walls as a canvas, converting commonplace locations into bright artworks. From charming marine animals to thought-provoking social criticism, each mural tells a tale about the island's diverse cultural past. Many of the town's most prominent murals can be found on Calle 3, Calle 6, and Avenida G. Don't forget to bring your camera to record these Instagrammable moments!

Indigenous crafts: For millennia, the indigenous people of Bocas del Toro have maintained their ancient craft practices, passing them down from generation to generation. From finely carved wooden masks to handwoven baskets embellished with bright designs, each piece reflects the artists' distinct ethnic identities.

- Visiting Indigenous Communities: To get a direct experience with indigenous crafts, consider visiting one of the native communities, such as the Ngäbe-Buglé villages of Salt Creek or Bastimentos.

You may watch artists at work, learn about their methods, and even buy original handmade mementos to take home.

- Craft Workshops and Classes: Those interested in getting hands-on with Bocas del Toro's art and craft traditions can try attending a workshop or class offered by local craftsmen. Whether you enjoy ceramics, painting, or traditional weaving, there is something for everyone to express their creativity. Check with local art galleries, cultural institutions, and community organizations about forthcoming workshops and programs. Many institutions provide beginner-friendly classes, which are ideal for tourists wishing to learn a new skill or art.

Some workshops to learn about art and craft traditions in Bocas del Toro include:

- Bocas Art School: Located in Bocas Town, the Bocas Art School provides a variety of courses and classes for tourists looking to explore their artistic side. From painting and drawing to ceramics and sculpture, there's something for everyone's artistic taste.

- Visit the Indigenous cultural center on Isla Bastimentos to take part in seminars offered by members of the Ngäbe-Buglé group. Learn ancient weaving skills, create exquisite beadwork, or try your hand at creating wooden masks with the help of professional artists.
- Casa Cultural: Located in the center of Bocas Town, Casa Cultural offers regular art and craft workshops led by local artists. Casa Cultural provides a pleasant environment for you to express your creativity, whether you enjoy photography, jewelry making, or mixed media.
- Red Frog Beach Resort: For a more immersive experience, stay at the Red Frog Beach Resort on Isla Bastimentos. The resort collaborates with local artists to offer seminars and lectures that teach guests traditional craft techniques while immersed in the island's natural splendor.

Tourists can immerse themselves in Bocas del Toro's art and craft traditions by taking workshop sessions at these recommended sites, where they will learn from professional artists and help the local community.

Getting to the core of Bocas del Toro's art and craft traditions is much easier than you might imagine. Bocas Town's cultural sites are easily accessible by foot, bicycle, or water taxi. For those traveling further out to visit Indigenous settlements, guided tours, and boat trips are offered to ensure a hassle-free experience.

Exploring Bocas del Toro's art and craft traditions entails not only viewing but also immersing oneself in the creative process and bonding with the local population. Whether you're trying your hand at pottery, admiring a mural, or learning about indigenous weaving skills, each encounter provides a window into the heart of this dynamic city.

So unleash your inner artist on a cultural tour through Bocas del Toro's colorful streets and hidden gems. Who knows. You might discover a newfound enthusiasm for creation that will last long after you leave our tropical paradise.

CHAPTER FIVE

Where to Stay and Dine

Welcome to Chapter 5 of your Bocas del Toro Travel Guide, where we will explore the wonderful world of accommodation and dining in this tropical paradise.

Accommodation Choices

Whether you're looking for luxurious, eco-friendly lodges or low-cost guesthouses, Bocas del Toro has a wide choice of options to fit any traveler's interests and preferences.

1. Hotel and Resort: For those looking for a luxurious hideaway with all the amenities of a home, go no further than the hotels and resorts sprinkled across Bocas del Toro. From beachside villas to boutique hotels in the middle of town, these lodgings provide luxury facilities, breathtaking views, and personalized service to make your stay special. After a day of seeing the islands, relax with spa treatments, gourmet dinners, and stylish accommodations.

2. Eco-Lodges: If you're interested in sustainability and eco-tourism, Bocas del Toro has a variety of eco-lodges that merge effortlessly into the natural surroundings. Immerse yourself in the splendor of the rainforest while living in eco-friendly lodgings that value conservation and community involvement. Wake up to the sound of birds singing, go on guided nature walks, and participate in eco-friendly activities that benefit the environment.

3. Hostels and Guesthouses: Traveling on a budget? Not a problem! Bocas del Toro has a thriving hostel and guesthouse industry, allowing backpackers and budget-conscious tourists to choose economical lodgings without compromising luxury or convenience. Whether you're seeking a dormitory-style hostel with a vibrant social environment or a tranquil guesthouse with individual rooms, there are plenty of alternatives available. Plus, staying in a hostel or guesthouse allows you to meet other visitors and share experiences and insights about your adventures in Bocas del Toro.

4. Bed and breakfasts: Staying at one of Bocas del Toro's quaint bed & breakfasts provides a more intimate and customized experience. These charming hotels are run by friendly residents who are passionate about sharing their love for the location. They provide warm hospitality, delicious breakfasts, and insider information on the finest places to visit. Before heading off for a day of adventure in Bocas del Toro, wake up to the aroma of freshly prepared coffee and baked pastries.

5. Vacation rentals: Have you been seeking a dwelling away from home? Consider renting a vacation house or apartment in Bocas del Toro to experience the independence and flexibility of having your place. Whether you're traveling with family, friends, or as a couple, vacation rentals allow you to prepare your meals, relax in large living rooms, and enjoy peace and seclusion away from the masses. Furthermore, many vacation accommodations provide breathtaking ocean views and convenient access to beaches and activities.

6. Camping: Camping in Bocas del Toro is a popular choice for adventurous souls who love to sleep under the sky. Pitch your tent on a quiet beach, in a thick jungle, or at a designated campsite and drift off to the calming sounds of nature. Camping allows you to immerse yourself in the natural splendor of Bocas del Toro and provides a unique opportunity to explore the location as a genuine adventurer. Whatever your budget, interests, or travel style, Bocas del Toro has a broad choice of lodging alternatives to meet your needs. This tropical paradise has something for everyone, from magnificent resorts to affordable hostels, and eco-friendly lodges to quaint bed and breakfasts.

Hotels & Resorts

1. Nayara Bocas del Toro: This hotel offers individual concierge service. Nayara Bocas del Toro features an outdoor swimming pool, a fitness center, a garden, and a communal lounge. This 5-star hotel has complimentary WiFi, room service, and a 24-hour front desk. The facility is a Smoke-free property that accepts Credit Cards and Debit cards and offers Spa services and free Breakfast. The facility offers continental, American, and vegetarian breakfast options. People may order a drink at the bar during their stay. The check-in time is usually 15:00 and the check-out time is noon. They are located at Isla Frangipani, Panama City. If you need to know more about their services, you can call; +1 844-865-2002.

I had the finest treehouse experience when I lodged at this hotel during one of my visits to Bocas del Toro. My room was spacious and had a private bathroom and balcony. Nayara Bocas del Toro offers bike rentals, so feel free to rent one if you want to explore the area. It is also important to note that pets are not allowed in the hotel. The cost of residing in this hotel per night depends on the room type. However, Double room all-inclusive rates begin at $1400 per night.

2. Punta Caracol Aqua-lodge: This rustic ecolodge on stilts overlooking the Caribbean Sea features thatched-roof wood bungalows with solar panels and is accessible by water taxi or aircraft. It is 6 km from the quiet Starfish Beach. The 9 bi-level, TV-free suites have sitting rooms with pull-out couches and patios with sea views. All provide Wi-Fi, safes, ceiling fans, and mosquito nets. Some have immediate sea access. Boat trips to and from the airport are free. There is an open-air restaurant and bar with a patio overlooking the sea. Breakfast, sightseeing, and loaner kayaks and snorkeling gear are also offered. Check-in time is noon and check-out time is Check-out time is 11:00. The hotel is pet-friendly and they also offer free Breakfast and Airport Shuttle services. You can contact them at +507 6461-2604 for more information. Prices normally begin around $132 per night.

3. Playa Tortuga Hotel and Beach Resort: This elegant resort in a complex overlooking the Caribbean Sea is 4 kilometers from Under Sea Panama, 7 kilometers from Playa Buff, and 14 kilometers from Starfish Beach. Sophisticated rooms and suites have complimentary Wi-Fi, cable TV, and balconies. The suites maintain living rooms and futon beds. A free transport to the town center is available. Dining choices include a casual diner near a pier, a snack bar, and a restaurant serving Panamanian and American cuisine. There's also an outdoor pool, a kids' pool, a kid's club, and a fitness center with a massage room. Kayaks, snorkeling equipment, and a volleyball court are all accessible. The Check-in time is 15:00 and the Check-out time is noon. The Address & Contact Information of the hotel are Isla Colon S/N, Bocas del Toro, Province of Bocas del Toro, Panama, and +507 757-9050 respectively. You can call to get more information and also make reservations. Prices begin at 186$ per night.

4. Tropical Suites Hotel: Tropical Suites is a contemporary beachside hotel situated in the center of Bocas del Toro. The resort, located on a calm Caribbean beachfront, is near to several over-the-water restaurants, shopping, and activities. The hotel's suites provide panoramic views of the Caribbean oceans or the island's tropical scenery. Amenities include private balconies, air conditioning, a 24-hour front desk, and access to the hotel's dock. Beaches, snorkeling, dolphin viewing, zip line, diving, and surfing are all nearby attractions. Tours and activities may be scheduled through the hotel's front desk. Guests may opt to include breakfast in their accommodation fee. The home is a 15-minute walk or a quick taxi ride from the Bocas Town Island airport. There is also Free High-Speed Internet (Wi-Fi) available in the rooms. Prices normally begin at $139.

5. La Coralina Island House: An oceanfront boutique hotel on Bocas del Toro's top surf break. This vast resort has a lush landscape and Bali-inspired architecture, as well as 23 guest rooms and 8 villas, a luxury spa and sauna, a fitness center, a yoga studio, an on-site full-service restaurant and bar, and three pools for guests to enjoy. Devoted bilingual support staff ready to fulfill all of your demands. Some benefits you will enjoy in this lodge include Free High-Speed Internet (Wi-Fi), a Fitness Center with a Gym and Workout Room, Free Breakfast, and Pets allowed especially dogs. This hotel is located at Ruta Principal A Bluff, Paunch, 10001 Panama. You can call 009 507 851-0800 for more information. Prices normally start around $310.

6. Roam Yoga and Wellness Lodge: This lodge is situated at Isla Solarte in Bocas del Toro, Panama, 200 meters from Carenero Beach. Captain Manuel Niño International Airport is 48 kilometers from the hotel as well. The lodge has lodging with a restaurant, private parking at no charge, a garden, and a balcony. The hotel offers family rooms. The hotel's rooms include balconies, a private bathroom with a bath, Tea/coffee maker, and free WiFi, with some rooms offering a view of the sea. The accommodations provide bed linen and towels. The daily breakfast includes vegetarian, vegan, and gluten-free alternatives. Roam Yoga & Wellness Lodge guests may participate in activities in and around Bocas del Toro, such as hiking and snorkeling. Check-in time is usually from 14:00 - 20:00.

Eco-Lodges

1. LA SELVA at Nomad Tree Lodge: LA SELVA at Nomad Tree Lodge is an off-grid eco-lodge ideal for surfers, yogis, and travelers of all types. The accommodation is a jungle treehouse community with a fresh new yoga shala, where you may join in for the daily jungle yoga practice. They also have a jungle pool where you may rest and relax after your travels or your day's itinerary. They are within walking distance to Paunch's world-class surf break (10-minute walk, intermediate/advanced wave), as well as Tiger Tail, an epic wave right at the end of their driveway. They also have a Bar/ Lounge within if you decide to have a cool time. The beach is located on Paunch Beach Road, at Beach Road 01, Isla Colon Bocas del Toro Province, Panama. You can reach them at +1 816-509-1451.

2. Bambuda Lodge: The Bambuda Lodge is the second option. This laid-back hostel, located on the beaches of Admiral's Bay in Isla Solarte, Panama, and surrounded by woodland, is 2 kilometers from Wizard's Beach and 5 kilometers from the Palagna ferry station. Simple dormitories and rooms with wood flooring have free Wi-Fi, ceiling fans, and communal amenities. Upgraded rooms include private bathrooms. There is a casual restaurant with open-air dining and sea views, as well as an outdoor pool with a patio and sun loungers. Some rooms include air conditioning. The Check-in time is 14:00 and the Check-out time is 11:00. You can call them at +1 786-789-4889. The cost of this eco-lodge usually begins at $68 per night.

3. Casa Cayuco Eco Adventure Lodge: Nestled on the edge of the woods, only steps from the beach. Their secluded setting allows people to genuinely getaway. This lodge thinks that the most crucial aspect of ecotourism is having a beneficial influence on local communities. A percentage of each stay at Casa Cayuco is being used by the lodge to support ongoing projects in the community. This facility has free High-Speed Internet (Wi-Fi), an on-site restaurant, a Yoga room, a Beach, a private balcony, a wardrobe/ closet, private restrooms, and a walk-in shower. They also offer free breakfast. This is also a family-friendly lodge as it has family rooms as well. This ecolodge is located in Punta Vieja, Isla Bastimentos 0101 Panama. The nearby attractions include Isla Zapatillas (4.2 miles), Parque Nacional Marino Isla Bastimentos (3.9 miles), and Cueva de Marcielagos (4.2 miles). They also provide airport transportation or shuttles to clients. However, it is important to inform them ahead of time to check the information. The check-in time is 10:00 and the check-out time is 10:00

4. Tranquilo Bay Eco Adventure Lodge: It is located at Bastimentos Island in Bocas del Toro Province, Panama. The Tranquilo Bay Eco Adventure Lodge is an all-inclusive resort in Bocas del Toro, Panama. You can make reservations or get more information by dialing (713)-589-6952. Amenities and services visitors can enjoy in this eco-lodge include; free Breakfast, free Wi-Fi, Air conditioning, free Airport Shuttle, Credit Cards, Debit cards, Cash Services Front Desk baggage storage, Concierge, full-service laundry, Coffee maker in rooms, private bathrooms, bathtub in some rooms Bathrooms Private bathroom, Bathtub in some rooms among others.

5. Island Plantation: Island Plantation is located 8 km/6 miles from the town center of Bocas on the main island, Bluff Beach, Isla Colon Panama. This intimate beach resort is located on one of Bocas' most beautiful and unspoiled beaches in front of the warm Caribbean ocean with a lush jungle backdrop, just 20 minutes by car from Bocas Town on the main island. Island Plantation provides Deluxe-King and Twin rooms with Bali-style bathrooms and terraces that surround the tiled, in-ground pool and all have beach views, an on-site fine dining restaurant, an Italian Pizza restaurant, and the famous Beach Bar which is right on the beach, a shuttle, and an ocean view jungle yoga platform with breathtaking views of the sea and jungle. This lodge also provides free High-Speed Internet (Wi-Fi), Pool, Free breakfast, a Mosquito net, Private check-in and check-out. Suites Prices start at $251 per night.

6. La Loma Jungle Lodge and Chocolate Farm: La Loma, which is only accessible by boat, is located in the heart of the Isla Bastimentos rainforest on a 55-acre property that stretches from the mangrove shores of Bahia Honda Bay through tropical forest and fruit tree groves to the highest point on the island, providing breathtaking views of the jungle and bay. Lush, nectar-rich gardens attract a broad range of unusual creatures. The property borders the beautiful National Marine Park, and lovely white sand beaches are only a short boat ride away. The property is 10 kilometers from Bocas Town and offers sea views. This facility is committed to environmental sustainability and community care. Each room features a private bathroom with a hot water shower, comfy mattresses with canopy mosquito nets, overhead fans, and furnishings made on-site using local materials. Breakfast, lunch, and supper are all included in the price of your stay, and the on-site organic gardens provide many of the ingredients for the meals. The property provides complimentary tours of the organic chocolate farm to tourists.

La Loma also offers snorkeling tours to the Zapatillas and forest walks. La Loma is only accessible by boat. They also provide visits to Red Frog Beach, which is ten minutes away. A boat journey to and from Isla Colon on the check-in and check-out dates is included. The region is excellent for birdwatching, kayaking, snorkeling, and hiking. Free WiFi is also available. You can check in from 16:00 to 17:30, and check out till 11:00. When you book, you may choose whether you want an early or late check-in or check-out time. Pets are allowed. There are no additional costs. The price per night starts at $355.

7. Up In The Hill: Beautiful and quiet cottage on Isla Bastimentos' highest hill, overlooking the Pantai surf break. Fully furnished with a kitchen, queen-sized bed, bed sofa, living room, veranda, and hot water shower. The cabin is solar-powered and has a rainwater collecting system. The cottage is located on an organic chocolate and tropical fruit farm, not far from Up in the Hill Coffee Shop. A 15-minute walk through magnificent tropical vegetation from the Caribbean village of Old Bank, and 20 minutes from the stunning Wizard Beach, which is great for surfing or lounging. The cottage is an excellent base for surf outings, hiking, or a peaceful getaway from it all. The Up in the Hill Coffee Shop serves delicious breakfasts, homemade pizzas, gnocchi, and organic salads. Staying Up in the Hill is a genuinely unique experience that allows you to combine luxury, healthy living, and adventure while getting away from it all.

Hostels and Guesthouses

1. Bambuda Bocas Town: It is located at Avenida H Norte, between Calles 5 and 6, Bocas del Toro, Panama.

Bambuda Bocas Town has a restaurant, bar, common lounge, and free WiFi. It is less than 1 km from Istmito and 2.4 kilometers from Y Griega Beach. Certain rooms at the hotel have balconies with sea views. Breakfast is served every day and includes continental, American, and vegan options. The nearest airport is Bocas del Toro Isla Colon International Airport, which is just a few feet from the hostel. They provide Free WiFi and allow pets at an extra fee. Check-in is from 15:00 until 22:00. Guests must produce a picture identification and credit card at check-in. Check-out is from 6:00 until 11:00. Prices normally begin around $16 per night.

2. Bastimentos Hill Guest House: It is located at Calle Principal Isla in Bocas del Toro, Panama. Bastimentos Hill Guest House in Bocas del Toro offers accommodations with a patio, a communal lounge, and a private beach area. This facility provides a restaurant, a central kitchen, room service, and accessible WiFi. The dormitory offers family suites. All rooms include a private bathroom with a shower, and some include a kitchenette with a fridge. You may play darts in the hostel. The nearest airport is Bocas del Toro Isla Colon International Airport, which is just a few feet from Bastimentos Hill Guest House. Check-in is from 14:00 to

20:30 and Check-out is from 7:00 until 11:00. Pets are not permitted. It costs $25 each night to stay in this hostel.

3. Hostal on the Sea: It is located in Bocas del Toro, Panama, on North Avenue between 6 and 7 Street. The Hostel provides lodging in Bocas Town. The property includes a private beach area and BBQ facilities. The hostel has a communal lounge. The hotel's guest rooms come equipped with a coffee machine. Hostal On The Sea's accommodations have a private bathroom and complimentary WiFi. Guests are usually provided with a toaster. Canoeing and other activities in and around Bocas Town are available to guests staying in Hostal on the Sea. It is also suitable for families as it has children's outdoor play equipment and an Indoor Play Area as well. Check-in time is from 13:00-19:00 while the Check-out time is from 6:00 until 11:00. The price each night begins at $15 per night.

4. El Jaguar: El Jaguar, located in Bocas del Toro at Old Bank, has a bar, a communal lounge, and complimentary WiFi. This unit has a communal kitchen and a sun deck. Staff on-site can arrange for a shuttle service. The nearest airport is Bocas del Toro Isla Colon International Airport, which is just a few feet from the hostel. There are hammocks and loungers along the jetty where you may rest and see the lagoon. There is a well-organized kitchen with large fridge freezers, and the staff is courteous and accommodating. The Check-in time is from 13:00 until 21:00 while the Check-out time is from 8:00 until 10:00. Prices begin at $26 per night.

5. Surfari Bocas: it is located at Avenue B between Calles 4 and 5, Bocas del Toro, Panama. This lodge has super nice staff, comfortable beds, plenty of space, a nice common area, good laundry service, supermarkets, and restaurants nearby. The location is excellent. Right in the center of town, yet on a quiet street. Surfari Bocas is located on Isla Colón. The facilities are simple, yet clean, and provide all you need. Surfari Bocas provides pet-friendly accommodations in Bocas Town. The rooms are air-conditioned and include a private bathroom with a hot water shower. Surfari Bocas offers complimentary WiFi throughout the hotel. The nearby surroundings include restaurants, pubs, the airport, and water taxis. It offers Private check-in and check-out. The Check-in time is from 15:00 until 19:00. Pets are permitted on request between 05:00 and 11:00 although charges may be applied. Guests must produce a picture identification and credit card at check-in. The pricing is 29 dollars per pet night.

6. Spanish by the Sea (Bocas): It is located at Calle 4ta Detras del Hotel Bahia, Bocas del Toro. Spanish by the Sea - Bocas is located one block from the seashore in Bocas del Toro and features a community kitchen and eating room, a garden, a hammock area, and free Wi-Fi. The Spanish by the Sea hostel offers both private rooms and dormitory beds, all of which have access to communal restrooms. There are private lockers accessible in the hostel. Guests can unwind in the community lounge. The on-site tour desk can organize kayak rentals and advise on what to do in Bocas del Toro. Swimming and snorkeling may be done within a 5-minute walk to Spanish by the Sea, while surfing lessons are only a 5-minute boat ride away. Bocas del Toro Airport is about 1 km away and a one-hour flight from Panama City.

The Check-in time is from 13:00 until 20:00 and the Check-out time is from 7:00 to 11:00, prices normally cost $34.

Dining Scene

Welcome to Bocas del Toro, where each meal is a gourmet journey to be explored. From delectable seafood delicacies to exotic tropical fruits, the eating scene here is as broad and dynamic as the island itself. Join us as we on a culinary trip through the tastes of Bocas del Toro.

10 Must-try Local Cuisine and Specialties

One of the pleasures of dining in Bocas del Toro is the opportunity to sample real Panamanian cuisine, which is influenced by a combination of indigenous, African, Spanish, and Caribbean flavors. Here are some must-try foods and delicacies to entice your taste buds:

1. Patacones: Begin your gastronomic tour with a dish of patacones, a popular Panamanian snack composed of fried plantains. These savory pleasures are formed with fried green plantains that are flattened and cooked until crispy before being topped with a variety of savory toppings including shredded chicken, beans, guacamole, cheese, and ceviche, for a pleasant and flavorful feast. It is Ideal for a fast snack or a filling supper on-the-go.

2. Ceviche: No vacation to Bocas del Toro is complete without trying the local ceviche, a delicious meal prepared with fresh fish marinated in lime juice, onions, peppers, and cilantro. Whether you favor shrimp, fish, or mixed seafood, ceviche is a must-try dish that wonderfully encapsulates the tastes of the Caribbean.

3. Rondon: For a taste of authentic Caribbean cuisine, try Rondon, a hearty stew cooked with coconut milk, yams, plantains, and a variety of fresh seafood such as fish, shrimp, and crab. This rich and savory dish is popular among both residents and visitors, particularly on chilly evenings.

4. Seafood Platter: With its diverse marine life, Bocas del Toro is a seafood enthusiast's dream. Enjoy a delicious seafood plate with grilled lobster, shrimp skewers, fried fish, and octopus ceviche, served with rice, plantains, and a zesty side of spicy sauce. It's the ideal way to experience the flavors of the sea in one delightful supper.

5. Tropical Fruits: Don't forget to indulge your sweet taste with a variety of tropical fruits indigenous to the region. Bocas del Toro has a plethora of fresh fruits that are brimming with flavor and nutrition, including juicy pineapple and creamy mango, tangy passion fruit, and refreshing watermelon.

6. Chicha: Finish your dinner with a cool glass of chicha, a traditional fermented maize beverage that indigenous populations in Panama have enjoyed for years. This somewhat sweet and tangy drink complements any meal and reflects Panama's rich cultural past.

7. Raspao: On a sweltering day, cool down with a refreshing raspao, a local favorite made from shaved ice covered with sweet syrups in a variety of flavors, including tart tamarind and sweet mango. Add a dash of lime for an added rush of flavor, and enjoy this frosty treat while exploring Bocas del Toro's neighborhoods.

8. Carimañolas: A popular Panamanian snack with a crispy surface and flavorful interior of ground beef, chicken, or cheese. Carimañolas served with sour salsa or spicy aji sauce are a popular comfort dish for both residents and visitors.

9. Bollos: Bollos is a popular Panamanian street snack consisting of maize dough wrapped in banana leaves and cooked until soft. They are usually served with a choice of fillings, such as shredded chicken, pig, or fish, and a side of pickled veggies.

10. Tamales de Pescado: Tacos de Pescado, or fish tacos, are a great way to start exploring Bocas del Toro's dynamic gastronomic scene. Grilled fresh fish is served in warm corn tortillas, topped with crisp cabbage, zesty salsa, and creamy avocado. El Pirata Taco, located on the seaside promenade, serves the greatest fish tacos in town. El Pirata is well-known for its fresh, tasty seafood and relaxed environment, making it an ideal setting for a casual dinner with a view.

Dining Tips and Etiquette

To make the most of your gastronomic experience in Bocas del Toro, remember the following recommendations and etiquette:

- Respect the Locals: Enjoy the relaxed island atmosphere and take your time tasting each meal. Talk to residents and restaurant workers to discover more about Bocas del Toro's food and culture.
- Try Something New: Don't be scared to move outside of your comfort zone and try dishes you've

never had before. You could find a new favorite dish or taste that you didn't know existed.

- Support Local Businesses: Choose locally-owned restaurants and cafes to support the community while also enjoying the freshest products supplied by surrounding farms and fishermen.

- Enjoy the Ambiance: Many restaurants in Bocas del Toro have spectacular waterfront views and open-air seating, allowing you to dine outside while taking in the island's natural beauty.

Every meal in Bocas del Toro is an opportunity to enjoy Panama's colorful flavors while also learning about the Caribbean's rich culinary legacy. From delicious seafood meals to exotic tropical fruits, the dining scene here will satisfy even the most sophisticated palates. So take a seat, dive in, and enjoy the tastes of Bocas del Toro; you will not be disappointed.

Recommended Restaurants and Cafes

1. Buena Vista: This Restaurant is located at Calle 3ra Calle Principal on the ocean, Isla Colón, Panama. They specialize in Caribbean, Latin, seafood, and international dishes as well as Vegetarian, Vegan, and Gluten-Free

Options. So if you're a vegetarian you have nothing to worry about. Breakfast, lunch, dinner, brunch, and drinks are served in this restaurant. During my stay at Bocas, I often visited this restaurant. I ate breakfast every morning and a couple of meals, and they were all delicious! The Caribbean scramble was the finest breakfast. The toast was excellent. Excellent coffee and nice personnel. It is also an excellent choice for lunch too. You can call them for more information using this number: +507 757-9035. Their opening hours are usually between
7:30 AM to 9:30 PM.

2. Leaf Eaters Café: This Cafe is Vegetarian Friendly and it's usually open from 11:30 AM - 4:00 PM. It is suitable for lunch and drinks. This cafe is located at First Street on Carenero Island, Bocas Town, Isla Colon, Panama. Their specialty includes drinks, seafood, international cuisines, Vegetarian, Vegan, and Gluten-Free Options. The place also ensures quick service at very cheap rates. The last time I was here, I had fish tacos and I must say it was delicious.

3. The view from Oasis: A beautiful restaurant located in Oasis Bluff Beach that serves lunch and dinner while providing spectacular views of Bluff Beach and the Caribbean Ocean. Weather permitting, you may have lunch and beverages on the beach at their Beach Lounge or on the Garden's open-air Deck. You'll also enjoy freshly cooked meals and beverages. For lunch, be sure to enjoy handmade soups, salads, sandwiches, and hot meals, including their best-selling soft shell tacos and homemade Green Thai Curry, as well as their legendary Lime Pie. All of these are freshly prepared and tailored to your taste. Their supper menu is diverse, with steaks, locally caught fish and seafood, pasta, vegetarian and vegan alternatives. No matter what you eat at this restaurant don't miss the Thai Lime Shrimp as it is very delicious. The prices of cuisines vary from dish to dish. However, prices may begin from $4 - $17 or more.

4. Renny Pizza: If you are craving pizza, this outlet is for you! Renny Pizza is situated at Avenida A, Isla Colon, Panama. This establishment is known for making sumptuous pizza. They provide lunch, dinner, delivery, takeout, reservations, seating, alcohol, a full bar, free wifi, and table service. They also have special diets such as vegetarian and vegan Options. During one of my visits to Renny's, I tried the pizza and margaritas. The taste was truly fantastic. Pizza prices range from $8 to $13. However, a family pizza cost $40.

5. Arboloco: This location is ideal for a dating night. It has a jungle setting. They specialize in Caribbean, Seafood, Central American, International, and Grill delicacies. Arboloco is situated on Bluff Beach Road, Isla Colon 0101 Panama. You may reach them at +507 6521-5844. However, make reservations and bring USD cash, as that is what is generally accepted here; credit cards are not accepted. You should try some of the excellent dishes such as prawns, curry eggplant, Key lime pie, filet, and tuna. They also feature a large drink variety (including cocktails) for people who enjoy drinking. You may have lunch, dinner, and drinks here.

6. Coco Fastronomy – (La Casa del BAPÉ): They specialize in Caribbean, Central American, and Vegetarian-Friendly Cuisines. Vegetarian and vegan options are not left out as well. It is located on Calle 2nda, within the Hotel Bocas Del Toro, Bocas Town, Isla Colon 11100 Panama. Call +507 6871-2323 or send an email to cocofastronomy@gmail.com. They specialize in delivery, and takeout, and have a full bar where they serve alcohol, wine, and beer. They also accept Mastercard, Visa, Digital Payments, Cash, and Credit Cards. Table Service, Free WiFi, outdoor seating, and highchairs are available. The use of wheelchairs is very pretty accessible in this area. Their menu includes fresh bread, a variety of sandwiches with different flavors, ceviche, coconut shrimp, tuna steak, and more. Overall, the prices are reasonable, and the service is excellent. Before ordering the main course or genuine meal, enjoy a snack by sampling a sandwich and a Pina Colada for roughly $15 with a tip.

7. Café del Mar: This cafe runs from 8:00 AM until 10:00 PM. They specialize in Caribbean, Latin, Central American, and Vegetarian-friendly dishes. Cafe del Mar, in Bocas del Toro, is a restaurant that respects local foods by not including any preserved products on its menu. They produce all of their sauces in-house with all-natural ingredients. So you'll go from a massive morning Burrito to a delicious Ceviche for dinner. It is situated on Calle 1A, Bocas Town, Isla Colon 507 Panama. You may reach them at +507 6776-8858 or via cafedelmarpty@gmail.com. They provide cereal, hamburgers, pancakes, risotto, coffee, fish filets, and drinks, among others. You may sample several smoothies and rum. Their cuisine is relatively priced or inexpensive. During my visit to this restaurant, I tasted the Caribbean Homelet, and the taste wowed me. You may also try pancakes with eggs and bacon; they have a nice taste.

Their Orange juice is natural. The environment was quite nice.

8. Pier 19 Restaurant:: Pier 19 Restaurant is currently open on the Divers Paradise Boutique Hotel's deck in Bocas Town, Isla Colon, Panama 0101. You can reach them; at +507 6656-3662, or email: fb@diversparadise.com. They specialize in International, Vegetarian, and Vegan foods. They're usually open from 7:30 AM until 10:00 PM. Their Lobster has a great taste. I'll advise you to have a bite of the shrimp tacos and ceviche. This restaurant is suitable for special events, romance, scenic views, bar scenes, and business meetings. Excellent meal and lounge. Prices of dishes typically range from $5 - $20.

The restaurant serves Afro-Caribbean-inspired breakfast, lunch, and supper, with vegetarian, vegan, and gluten-free options. Pier 19 is a great addition to the Bocas restaurant scene, with beautiful sunsets over the marina and mainland, as well as special events like weekly jazz evenings and Sunday Caribbean Sunset. Expect pleasant people, tasty cuisine, and a fantastic atmosphere. Octopus and tuna are highly recommended. They also offer an excellent PADI-certified diving facility, so you can explore the underwater Bocas del

Toro. You may test it out. Pier 19 is attractive without being overly pricey.

Bocas del Toro's street food culture exemplifies the region's rich culinary heritage, with recipes passed down through generations and tastes that represent the many ethnic influences that have influenced Panama's cuisine. Every taste, from savory empanadas loaded with delicate meat and aromatic spices to crunchy plantain chips topped with zesty salsa, is a narrative of tradition and invention.

Navigating the Street Food Scene

Exploring Bocas del Toro's street food scene is an adventure unto itself, with bustling markets, vibrant food booths, and colorful carts lining the streets at every turn. To maximize your gastronomic trip, here are a few pointers for navigating the street food scene like a pro:

- Follow Your Nose: Allow your senses to guide you through the streets of Bocas del Toro, following the seductive odors of sizzling meats, frying empanadas, and boiling stews to uncover hidden gastronomic treasures.

- Accept the Chaos: Street food vendors might be packed, hectic, and bursting with activity, but don't let that put you off. Embrace the hustle and bustle, start up a discussion with the friendly vendors, and soak in the colorful spirit of the street food scene.

- Try Everything: One of the benefits of researching street food is the ability to try a broad range of foods without breaking the wallet. Don't be scared to try something new, get out of your comfort zone, and enjoy the distinct flavors of Bocas del Toro's street cuisine delights.

- Eat Like a Local: Locals are the most knowledgeable about street cuisine. Follow their lead and look for the stalls with the longest queues, largest crowds, and most excited customers. Most likely, you'll discover some of the tastiest meals

- Save Room for Dessert: No street food journey is complete without sampling a sweet treat or two. From rich churros coated with cinnamon sugar to creamy coconut flan, Bocas del Toro has a tantalizing selection of desserts to satiate your sweet taste and cap off your gastronomic tour on a high note.

Embark on a gastronomic tour through Bocas del Toro's colorful streets and discover a world of flavor, tradition, and innovation that awaits exploration. From savory appetizers to sweet delicacies, the city's street food industry has something for everyone, providing a memorable culinary experience that will leave you wanting more. So grab a fork, and a stool, and prepare to enjoy the enticing delicacies of Bocas del Toro's street food culture Province.

Nightlife Hotspots

1. Floating Bar: Enjoy a day floating with us at The Floating Bar in Bocas del Toro, Panama. Come sip excellent drinks, eat amazing tacos, and take in the sights both above and below the water. Daily specials and happy hours are available from 12 noon to 2 p.m. Service choices include outside seats. Serves delicious drinks. Do not take bookings. Price per person: PAB 10-15.

2. Tequila Republic: Service choices include happy-hour meals. They serve tasty drinks and the area is good for viewing sports. It is located at Avenue E Nte., Bocas del Toro, Panama. It usually opens at 2 pm. You can reach out to them at; +507 6554-1563. The only tequila bar in Bocas! Happy Hour every hour, artisan cocktails, delicious cuisine, ice cold beer, and the greatest assortment of liquor is their specialty. Their building has two stories; please keep in mind that they are on the LOWER floor, and the upper level is occupied by another institution.

3. Lost Boys Blues Bar: This bar offers amazing beverages and live acts. Cuisines are also served at the bar. They are situated at 8QX9+Q38, Isla Carenero Sentero, Bocas del Toro, Provincia de Bocas del Toro, Panama. You can reach them for more information at +507 6887-1813. The perfect venue to listen to fantastic music. The only site on the island with the finest acoustics and rock! Incredible. Impressive recording studio on an island in Bocas del Toro, as well as a lovely bar where you can listen to great local and international musicians! Ideal for having a couple of beers with pals.

Boca's has more than enough to offer, whether you are a foodie, love arts or music, Bocas del Toro is suitable

CHAPTER SIX

Shopping and Souvenirs

Welcome to the bustling shopping scene in Bocas del Toro! Whether you're seeking one-of-a-kind mementos to

remember your vacation or the ideal present to take home, this tropical paradise has a plethora of shopping options for you.

Prepare to go on a shopping journey unlike any other as we take you through the top retail districts and marketplaces in Bocas del Toro. From lively street markets to lovely shops, there's something for everyone's taste and budget.

1. Shambala: This shop offers things for the mind, body, and spirit, as well as the most unusual presents and treasures. They have crystals, incense, diffusers, wooden puzzles, yoga mats, tarot and oracle cards, and much more. They are on 2nd Street, beside the white municipal building. Blue skyscraper with a large neon Shambala name. They are usually open from 10:00 AM - 5:30 PM.

2. Bocas Store Market: For a more varied shopping experience, visit Bocas Store Market, a unique bazaar packed with handcrafted products and old treasures. Browse a diverse selection of apparel, accessories, and home décor products, each with its unique tale to tell. Whether you're looking for a one-of-a-kind piece for your wardrobe or a unique memento to bring home, Bocas Store Market offers something for everyone. situated on Av. F Nte. 40-1 in Bocas del Toro, Panama.

Insider tip: Visit the Mercado de Mariscos (market) for seafood.

3. Boca Town: Begin your shopping adventure in the center of Bocas del Toro, Bocas Town. This dynamic area is home to a diverse range of businesses and boutiques selling anything from handcrafted crafts to designer goods. Take a stroll down the seaside promenade, where you'll discover a variety of sellers offering colorful sarongs, hand-carved wooden trinkets, and local jewelry.

Don't miss out on exploring the vibrant Main Street, which is dotted with quaint stores selling anything from handmade chocolates to hand-painted pottery. Make sure to visit the local markets, where you may taste fresh fruits, vegetables, and fish or buy ingredients for a tasty home-cooked supper.

4. Isla Colón: Travel beyond Bocas Town to the lovely island of Isla Colón, where you can find even more shopping opportunities. Visit the historic Bocas Marina, where you can explore a variety of boutique stores selling anything from boho apparel to handcrafted leather products.

Explore the busy street markets that dot Isla Colón to get a sense of local flavor. You'll discover an unusual mix of sellers offering handcrafted fabrics, traditional crafts, and freshly cooked street cuisine. Take your time exploring the maze of stalls, taking in the sights, sounds, and fragrances of this bustling market scene.

5. Bastimento Island: To have a genuinely unique shopping experience, take a water taxi to Bastimentos Island. This picturesque island is home to a bustling artisan community, where you can buy a wide variety of handcrafted products created by local craftsmen. Explore the vibrant alleyways of Old Bank Village, where you'll discover charming stores and galleries displaying the work of brilliant artists and craftspeople. From elaborately woven fabrics to hand-carved wooden masks, each piece reflects Bocas del Toro's rich cultural past.

Tip: Bring Cash: Although many stores and markets in Bocas del Toro take credit cards, it's usually a good idea to have some cash on hand, especially when shopping at smaller vendors or street markets.

Tips for Bargaining

Ah, bargaining: the age-old practice of haggling over pricing at markets and bazaars all around the world. Whether you're a seasoned traveler or a first-time explorer, learning the art of bargaining may help you save money while also adding excitement to your shopping experience. Grab your bargaining cap and prepare to negotiate like a pro with these insider tips from the streets of Bocas del Toro.

- **Understanding The Culture of Bargaining:** Before we get into the details of negotiating, it's important to understand the cultural environment of Bocas del Toro. Bargaining is a popular activity across Panama, particularly at local markets and street sellers. It's not only about obtaining the greatest bargain; it's also about developing rapport and connecting with the seller. So, embrace the spirit of negotiation with an open mind and a kind demeanor.

- **Do your research:** The key to effective negotiation is information. Before you begin bargaining, spend some time researching the typical pricing of the things you're interested in. This will provide you with a starting point from which you may establish a realistic offer. Remember that pricing might fluctuate based on aspects such as quality, workmanship, and demand, so be prepared to alter your expectations appropriately.

- **Start with a smile:** When haggling in Bocas del Toro, maintaining a nice manner might help. Begin by welcoming the merchant with a friendly grin and courteous welcome. This creates a nice tone for the discussion and demonstrates that you are personable and respectful. Remember that negotiation is more about developing connections than it is about getting a good deal.

- **Know Your Limits:** While negotiating may be enjoyable, it is critical to understand and adhere to your boundaries. Before you begin bargaining, determine the highest price you are willing to pay for the item. This can help you stay focused and avoid becoming caught up in the thrill of the moment. If the seller is unable to meet your price, don't be scared to walk away; there are plenty of other merchants looking to make a transaction.

- **Be prepared to walk away:** One of the most effective negotiation strategies is the courage to walk away. If the vendor is unwilling to meet your price, do not be afraid to gently refuse their offer and begin to walk away. This frequently prompts the vendor to decrease their price or make a counteroffer to keep you engaged. Remember that negotiation is a two-way street, and often the best offer is the one you don't take.

- **Stay Calm and Negotiate:** Negotiating may be an emotional experience, but it is critical to remain cool and controlled during the process. Avoid being angry or irritated, as lthey might impair your capacity to think clearly and make sound judgments. Instead, concentrate on conveying your offer straightforwardly and courteously, and be willing to listen to the seller's viewpoint. Remember that negotiating is a discussion, not a conflict, so keep the conversation positive and helpful.

- **Bundle your purchases:** Another good negotiation approach is to group your items. If you are purchasing many things from the same vendor, attempt to negotiate a cheaper price for the entire bundle. Sellers are frequently more ready to provide discounts when they anticipate a greater sale, so take advantage of this opportunity to save even more money on your purchases.

- **Know when to walk away**: As much as we want to save money on every purchase, it's not always possible. If the vendor refuses to meet your price or you are dissatisfied with the parameters of the discussion, it is OK to walk away. Remember, there are many other suppliers out there, and you're likely to find what you're searching for elsewhere. Don't allow a failed negotiation to spoil your shopping experience; instead, use it as an opportunity to find new possibilities and hidden gems.

- **Express gratitude:** Finally, whether or not you reach an agreement, remember to thank the vendor. Thank them for their time and thought, and let them know you value their willingness to compromise. Building great connections with sellers will pay dividends in the long term, so take the time to express your gratitude for their efforts.

Bargaining is an art form that requires time and experience to perfect, but with these insider secrets from Bocas del Toro, you'll be well on your way to being a skilled negotiator. So, the next time you're perusing the Bocas del Toro markets, remember to smile, remain cool, and negotiate confidently. Happy bargaining!

Souvenir Ideas

After basking in the sun, exploring secret coves, and immersing yourself in the lively culture of Bocas del Toro, it's time to take a bit of paradise home with you. Souvenir shopping in Bocas del Toro is an experience in and of itself, with a plethora of unique artifacts to be discovered. Whether you're looking for homemade crafts, local artwork, or classic items, there's something for everyone's taste and budget. So take your shopping bag and let's go on a quest to locate the right gifts to remember your stay in Bocas del Toro.

1. Handmade Crafts: As you travel through the bright streets of Bocas del Toro, you'll be fascinated by the brilliant assortment of handcrafted items that line the pavements and fill the bustling marketplaces. From delicate fabrics to complex jewelry, the artistry of local artists is simply breathtaking. In this tour, we'll take you on a journey through Bocas del Toro's handcrafted crafts scene, where each piece offers a tale of tradition, ingenuity, and love. Here are ten unique handcrafted crafts you may find in Bocas del Toro.

- **Molas:** These elaborately woven tapestries are created by indigenous Guna women. Molas have brilliant patterns inspired by nature and ancient traditions, giving them a distinct and colorful addition to any house.
- **Tagua Nut Carvings:** Local artists cut tagua nuts, often known as vegetable ivory, into exquisite sculptures and jewelry pieces. Tagua nut carvings range from little creatures to intricate necklaces,

demonstrating the skill and inventiveness of Bocas del Toro artisans.

- **Beaded Jewelry:** Indigenous artists expertly weave bright beads into exquisite necklaces, bracelets, and earrings. Each bead is meticulously selected and placed to produce visually appealing designs that mirror the beauty of Bocas del Toro's natural surroundings.

- **Creations using Coconut Shells:** With so many coconuts on the islands, residents have mastered the technique of making coconut shell masterpieces. From carved bowls and cups to delicately patterned jewelry, these eco-friendly items are both gorgeous and long-lasting.

- **Wooden Masks:** Hand-carved wooden masks are a popular art form in Bocas del Toro, frequently utilized in cultural festivities and celebrations. These beautifully constructed masks are decorated with bright colors and significant motifs that depict legendary animals and ancestral spirits.

- **Sea Shell Art:** Beachcombers collect shells from the beaches of Bocas del Toro and turn them into wonderful works of art. Seashell art, ranging from elaborate mosaics to tiny sculptures, evokes the beauty of the sea and brings a bit of seaside appeal to any environment.

- **Handwoven Hammocks:** Hammocks are a mainstay of Caribbean culture, and Bocas del Toro is famous for its handcrafted hammocks constructed of natural fibers. These comfy and sturdy hammocks are available in a range of sizes and patterns, allowing you to rest in style.

- **Panama Hats:** Despite common assumptions, Panama hats originated in Ecuador, and they are abundantly available in Bocas del Toro. These skillfully woven hats are constructed of toquilla straw and are valued for their lightweight and breathable properties.

- **Ceramic Pottery:** Local artists make stunning ceramic pottery utilizing ancient skills passed down through generations. Ceramic pottery in Bocas del Toro ranges from hand-painted tiles to sculptural vases, reflecting the region's rich cultural legacy.

- **Hand-Painted Textiles:** Textile artisans in Bocas del Toro paint elaborate motifs on fabric to create vivid tapestries, tablecloths, and apparel. These one-of-a-kind fabrics frequently incorporate themes inspired by local flora and animals, lending a tropical flare to any house.

- **Handcrafted Woven Baskets:** Visit local marketplaces and stores to find exquisitely woven baskets created by indigenous artists. These baskets come in a variety of sizes and patterns, making them ideal for keeping trinkets or exhibiting as beautiful items throughout your house.

Each of these unique handmade items provides a look into Bocas del Toro's rich cultural tapestry, making them valuable keepsakes for visitors and treasures for future generations.

2. Local Hot Sauce: Add a bottle of Bocas del Toro's locally manufactured hot sauce to your meals at home. These spicy sauces, made with fresh ingredients and strong spices, are ideal as souvenirs for both foodies and spice connoisseurs

3. Chocolate goods: Enjoy the taste of Bocas del Toro with chocolate goods created from locally cultivated cocoa beans. Indulge in handcrafted chocolate bars, cocoa nibs, or hot cocoa mix to experience the rich and luscious tastes of the Caribbean.

Local artwork at Bocas del Toro

Welcome to the vibrant world of local art in Bocas del Toro, where creativity knows no limitations and every brushstroke tells a tale. As you walk through the streets of this dynamic archipelago, you'll come across a plethora of artistic expressions that represent the region's rich culture and natural beauty. Bocas del Toro is a refuge for art fans seeking inspiration and authenticity, with breathtaking paintings and complex handicrafts, as well as dramatic performances and immersive experiences.

Explore Artisan Workshops and Galleries

One of the finest ways to immerse yourself in Bocas del Toro's art scene is to visit the archipelago's numerous artisan studios and galleries. Here, you may meet local artists and craftspeople, learn about their creative processes, and even try your hand at creating your masterpiece. From ancient skills passed down through generations to cutting-edge modern art, Bocas del Toro provides an intriguing peek into the world of Panamanian creativity.

Here's some local artwork:

- Driftwood Sculptures: Local artisans in Bocas del Toro use driftwood from the beaches to create magnificent sculptures influenced by sea life and Caribbean culture. These sculptures represent the beauty of nature and the significance of conservation. They may be found and purchased at Bocas Town's art galleries and seaside shops, as well as along the shores of other islands.

- Coconut Shell Jewelry: Local craftsmen in Bocas del Toro create one-of-a-kind jewelry items out of coconut shells, which are typically embellished with beads, shells, and other natural materials. These jewelry items represent sustainability and the beauty of Caribbean craftsmanship. They may be bought in souvenir stores and artisan markets in Bocas Town and the surrounding areas.

- Seashell Wind Chimes: Wind chimes constructed from seashells found on the beaches of Bocas del Toro provide calming tones that recall the tranquility of island life. These wind chimes represent harmony with nature and may be found hanging outside coastal cafés, businesses, and artisan enterprises around the archipelago.

- Original paintings: Local painters have created bright seascape paintings that highlight the splendor of Bocas del Toro's coastal settings. These paintings, which represent the region's natural beauty, are frequently shown at art galleries and studios in Bocas Town. Visitors may take home a bit of paradise by purchasing original paintings or prints.

- Rainforest ceramics: In Bocas del Toro, artisans produce ceramics inspired by the beautiful jungles that surround the archipelago. These clay pieces frequently include elaborate leaf and flower themes that represent the bounty of nature. Rainforest pottery may be obtained at pottery workshops and artisan fairs in Bocas Town and the surrounding areas.

- Recycled Metal Sculptures: In Bocas del Toro, local artisans reuse scrap metal to create innovative sculptures that symbolize sustainability and environmental conscience. These sculptures may be seen along the waterfront promenade in Bocas Town, as well as at art galleries and outdoor markets around the archipelago.

- Traditional Bocas Town Murals: Colorful murals decorate the walls of buildings in Bocas Town, depicting images from local life, history, and folklore. These paintings capture the colorful culture and communal spirit of Bocas del Toro. Visitors may find these murals by taking self-guided walking tours through Bocas Town's streets and alleyways.

- Banana Leaf Art: Local craftsmen in Bocas del Toro weave elaborate motifs from banana leaves, creating stunning works of art that represent the region's tropical lushness and biodiversity. These works may be purchased in artisan markets and eco-lodges around the archipelago, demonstrating the local artists' sustainable and environmentally beneficial techniques.

- Hand-Painted Surfboards: Inspired by the lively surf culture of Bocas del Toro, local artisans convert surfboards into one-of-a-kind works of art. Each board is hand-painted with a variety of vibrant themes, including abstract patterns, marine life, and tropical landscapes. These beautiful surfboards are on display at Bocas Town's beachside cafés, surf stores, and art galleries.

Exploring Traditional Products in Bocas del Toro

Welcome to Bocas del Toro, where the colorful culture matches the natural beauty that surrounds it. One of the most enjoyable elements of touring this tropical paradise is finding its traditional items, each a one-of-a-kind gem that embodies the region's past and artistry. Join us on a tour through Bocas del Toro's markets, boutiques, and artisan workshops to discover the traditional goods that make this resort so unique.

1. Cacao, the Food of the Gods: Our first destination on our voyage will be the world of cocoa, a precious substance venerated by indigenous civilizations for ages. Bocas del Toro is home to beautiful cocoa plantations, where farmers meticulously nurture this valuable commodity. Take a tour of a cacao farm to learn about the farming process and try freshly roasted cocoa. For a decadent experience, try handmade chocolate handcrafted in Bocas del Toro. From dark and velvety to creamy and indulgent, you'll find a world of tastes to satisfy your palate and feed your spirit.

2. Handcrafted Jewelry: No vacation to Bocas del Toro is complete without experiencing the island's wonderful handcrafted jewelry. Local craftsmen are inspired by the natural beauty of their surroundings, adding vivid gemstones, shells, and pearls into their masterpieces. Wander around Bocas Town's lively markets and boutique stores to find a stunning selection of earrings, necklaces, and bracelets that mirror the hues of the Caribbean Sea. Each item offers a tale about the water, the sun, and the spirit of Bocas del Toro, making it an ideal keepsake to keep for years.

3. Panama hats: Despite its name, Panama hats originated in Ecuador, but they have since become synonymous with flair and refinement in Panama and beyond. Panama hats are made from the finest toquilla straw and handmade by expert craftsmen utilizing skills passed down through centuries. Take a trip along Bocas Town's waterfront promenade, where sellers sell an outstanding array of Panama hats in a range of shapes and colors. Whether you choose a classic fedora or a wide-brimmed sun hat, you'll find the ideal Panama hat to complete your island look.

4. Handwoven Textiles: Step into the world of traditional Panamanian textiles, where brilliant colors and complex patterns combine to produce works of art that are both beautiful and utilitarian. Handwoven textiles are a vital part of everyday life in Bocas del Toro, ranging from brilliantly colored hammocks that sway softly in the breeze to elaborately woven baskets ideal for keeping treasures. Visit a local artisan workshop to observe experienced weavers in action and learn about the traditional processes used to manufacture these gorgeous items. Whether you're seeking home décor or the ideal present, you'll find a lovely collection of handwoven textiles to pick from.

Immerse yourself in Bocas del Toro's lively art culture, where creativity knows no boundaries and inspiration awaits around every turn. Local artwork reflects the numerous cultural influences that define this one-of-a-kind location, ranging from vibrant paintings that capture the beauty of the islands to quirky sculptures that celebrate the Caribbean spirit. Explore Bocas Town's galleries and studios to find a wide range of creative styles and materials, including traditional oil paintings and modern mixed-media works. Whether you're an experienced art collector or simply admire beauty in all its forms, Bocas del Toro is guaranteed to have something that calls to you.

As we conclude our tour through Bocas del Toro's traditional items, we hope you have been encouraged to discover the rich cultural tapestry of this fascinating place. From the earthy taste of cocoa to the timeless beauty of

Panama hats, each traditional product reflects Bocas del Toro's workmanship, heritage, and colorful attitude. So, whether you're sampling delectable chocolates or admiring the beautiful weaving of handcrafted cloth, take a minute to appreciate the beauty and creativity that surrounds you in this tropical paradise.

CHAPTER SEVEN

Practical Tips and Advice

When touring the breathtaking archipelago of Bocas del Toro, it is critical to have access to dependable resources and emergency connections. While this tropical paradise is renowned for its beauty and tranquility, unexpected events sometimes occur. Knowing who to contact may make a big difference when you need medical care, legal counsel, or just a helping hand. Here's a full list of helpful resources and emergency contacts in Bocas del Toro:

Emergency Services

In case of an emergency, call 911 for urgent help. Bocas del Toro's emergency services are well-equipped to deal with a variety of scenarios, including medical crises and natural catastrophes. When asking for assistance, ensure that you offer clear and precise information about your location and the nature of the problem.

1. Medical Assistance: If you want medical help during your stay in Bocas del Toro, various healthcare institutions can give skilled treatment. The Hospital Regional de Bocas del Toro is the area's principal hospital, with modern facilities and qualified medical personnel. In addition to the hospital, clinics, and pharmacies are available across the archipelago for non-emergency medical needs.

Hospital Regional de Bocas del Toro Address: Avenida E, Bocas Town Phone Number: +507 757-9184.

2. Police and Law Enforcement: If you require police help or law enforcement action, please call the Bocas del Toro police department. The National Police of Panama (Policía Nacional de Panamá) maintains law and order in the region, assuring the safety of both inhabitants and tourists.

National Police of Panama (Bocas del Toro Station) Address: Calle 4ta, Bocas Town Phone Number: +507 757-9916.

3. Tourist Information Centers: If you need help or information during your vacation to Bocas del Toro, the tourist information centers are a great resource. These facilities are staffed by informed residents and tourist experts who can assist you with maps, brochures, and insider advice to help you make the most of your time in the archipelago.

Tourist Information Center (Bocas Town) Address: Avenida G, Bocas Town Phone: +507 757-9778.

4. Embassies and Consulates: Travelers in need of consular assistance or emergency services from their home country should be aware of the location and contact information for their nation's embassy or consulate in Panama. These diplomatic posts may help with passport concerns, legal matters, and emergency evacuation services if needed.

- Address: Clayton Building 783, Avenida Demetrio Basilio Lakas, Ancon, Panama City. Phone: +507 317-5000.
- Canadian Embassy (Panama City) Address: Piso 18, Calle 50, Panama City Phone: +507 294-2500
- United Kingdom Embassy (Panama City): Calle 53 Este, Obarrio, Panama City Phone: +507 297-6400

5. Local Assistance and Support: In addition to professional emergency services and government agencies, Bocas del Toro has several local organizations and community groups that may help and support inhabitants and guests. These groups may provide services such as language interpretation, transportation help, and humanitarian relief.

By being acquainted with these helpful services and emergency contacts in Bocas del Toro, you may travel with confidence and peace of mind, knowing that assistance is always just a phone call away. So pack your luggage, set out on your trip, and be certain that you're well-prepared for whatever the road may bring.

Useful Websites & Apps

1. VisitBocas.com: The one-stop store for everything Bocas del Toro. This extensive website provides up-to-date information on activities, lodging, food, and more. Whether you're planning your schedule or seeking last-minute suggestions, VisitBocas.com has you covered.

2. Tripadvisor.com: With millions of traveler ratings and comments, TripAdvisor is an excellent resource for discovering the finest of Bocas del Toro. Browse top-rated hotels, restaurants, and activities, as well as read real-life experiences from other travelers, to help you confidently plan your trip.

3. LonelyPlanet.com: Known for its excellent travel recommendations, Lonely Planet's website contains a wealth of information about Bocas del Toro. From detailed trip itineraries to travel tips and advice, you'll learn all you need to know to traverse this tropical paradise like an expert.

4. BocasBreeze.com: The Bocas Breeze website provides information about local events, news, and activities in Bocas del Toro. Whether you're interested in cultural events, community projects, or environmental conservation efforts, Bocas Breeze knows what's going on in the archipelago.

5. Bocas.com: This locally owned website provides insider information and suggestions from Bocas del Toro inhabitants. Discover hidden jewels, off-the-beaten-path sights, and real cultural experiences that are not covered in standard tourist guides.

6. Google Maps: You can easily navigate Bocas del Toro with the Google Maps app. From navigating the islands to identifying nearby restaurants and sights, Google Maps is your go-to guide for enjoying this tropical paradise.

7. Uber: Need a ride in Bocas del Toro? The Uber app makes transportation simple and convenient. Simply order a ride with the touch of a button and enjoy economical transportation wherever your activities lead you.

8. WhatsApp: The WhatsApp messaging software allows you to stay in touch with friends, family, and fellow travelers. Share photographs, plan meetups, and swap travel advice in real-time to ensure you never miss out on a memorable occasion in Bocas del Toro.

9. The XE Currency Converter app: This app lets you keep track of currency exchange rates. Whether you're shopping for souvenirs or dining at a local restaurant, this helpful software can help you manage and organize your costs.

10. The Weather Underground app: This app can help you stay up to date on the weather in Bocas del Toro. Get real-time temperature, humidity, and precipitation forecasts so you can confidently plan your outdoor outings.

Allow these recommended websites and applications to be your digital companions while exploring Bocas del Toro. These online resources will help you organize your schedule and navigate the islands, ensuring that your journey is seamless and unforgettable. So download your favorite applications, bookmark your favorite websites, and prepare to experience the wonder of Bocas del Toro like never before.

Sample Itineraries for Every Traveler

Are you ready for an exciting adventure through the lovely archipelago of Bocas del Toro? Whether you're a beach bum, an adventurer, or a cultural vulture, we've created the ideal schedule to make the most of your stay in this tropical paradise. Prepare to dive into crystal-clear seas, explore beautiful jungles, and immerse yourself in the colorful local culture. Let's go explore Bocas del Toro together!

Beach Lovers' Paradise

Day 1: Arrival and Beach Relaxation

- Arrive at Bocas del Toro and settle into your beachside accommodations.
- Spend the afternoon relaxing on the pure white beaches of Playa Bluff. Take a nice plunge in the turquoise waters, soak up the sun, and listen to the soft lapping of the waves.

Day 2: Island-hopping Adventure

- Go on an island-hopping tour of the Bocas del Toro archipelago. Visit the breathtaking Isla Zapatilla, where you can dive among bright coral reefs and swim with unusual aquatic creatures.

- Explore Isla Bastimentos' isolated beaches, including the famed Red Frog Beach. Keep an eye out for the renowned red poison dart frogs that inhabit this island.

Day 3: Surf's up!

- Rise early and travel to Bocas del Toro's surf destination, Playa Paunch. Whether you're an experienced surfer or a beginner, there are waves for everyone. Grab a board and hit the waves for a thrilling morning of surfing.

- After working up an appetite, enjoy a seaside lunch at one of the local surf shacks. Feast on fresh seafood and refreshingly cool beverages while taking in the Caribbean's laid-back ambiance.

The Adventure Seeker's Expedition

Day One: Rainforest Trekking

- Lace up your hiking boots and explore the magnificent jungle that surrounds Bocas del Toro.

Join a guided rainforest hike to see secret waterfalls, old caverns, and unusual species.

- Keep a watch out for howler monkeys, sloths, and toucans as you travel through the deep forest. Don't forget to bring lots of water and food to sustain your expedition!

Day Two: Underwater Exploration

- Dive into the beautiful waters of Bocas del Toro for a day of snorkeling and scuba diving. Explore vivid coral gardens, underwater tunnels, and sunken shipwrecks rich in marine life.

- Join a guided diving excursion to some of the archipelago's top dive spots, including the well-known Hospital Point and Coral Garden. Swim among colorful fish, marine turtles, and the odd hammerhead shark.

Day 3: Zip Line Thrills

- A zipline trip under the jungle canopy will get your adrenaline-pounding. Strap on and fly through the trees on a variety of thrilling zip lines, hanging bridges, and Tarzan swings.

- Enjoy panoramic vistas of the beautiful forest below as you fly from platform to platform. Don't forget to take some amazing selfies to remember your flying trip!

Culture Explorer's Journey

Day 1: Cultural immersion

- A visit to the indigenous Ngäbe-Buglé village allows you to immerse yourself in Bocas del Toro's vivid culture. Interacting with local artists allows you to learn about traditional customs, rituals, and workmanship.

- Join a hands-on session to make traditional handicrafts including woven baskets, beaded jewelry, and wooden sculptures. Take home a piece of Bocas del Toro's rich cultural legacy as a memento of your visit.

Day Two: Culinary Delights

- Take a gastronomic journey through the lively streets of Bocas Town. Sample a variety of delectable delicacies inspired by Afro-Caribbean, Latin American, and indigenous Ngäbe-Buglé cuisines.

- Enjoy native delights like ceviche, patacones, and coconut-infused fish dishes. Wash it all down with a cool glass of chicha de Sapo, a typical Panamanian drink made from fermented maize.

Day 3 - Sunset Serenade

- Finish your cultural experience with a sunset serenade on a traditional wooden boat. Set sail along the peaceful waters of Bocas del Toro while listening to live music played by local artists.
- As the sun sets and the sky turns pink, orange, and gold, sip tropical drinks and eat gourmet appetizers. It's an ideal approach to conclude your cultural journey of Bocas del Toro.

Whatever sort of visitor you are, Bocas del Toro offers something special for you. So pack your bags, put your cares behind them, and prepare to go on an unforgettable vacation in this tropical paradise!

CONCLUSION

As your stay in Bocas del Toro draws to an end, it's natural to experience a range of emotions, from regret at leaving this tropical paradise to thankfulness for the memorable memories you've created. But don't worry, the charm of Bocas del Toro will last long after you've gone home.

Reflections on Your Journey

Take a minute to reflect on your travels to Bocas del Toro. Perhaps you've spent leisurely days reclining on sun-kissed beaches, soaking up the Caribbean heat and cooling off in crystal-clear seas. Perhaps you've explored the beautiful rainforest, found secret waterfalls, and met unusual creatures along the way. Perhaps you've immersed yourself in the colorful local culture, relishing the tastes of traditional food and dancing to the rhythms of live music.

Whatever adventures you've been on, one thing is certain: Bocas del Toro has left an unforgettable impression on your spirit. Its beauty, charm, and energy have all knitted themselves into the fabric of your being, becoming an integral part of who you are.

Be Thankful for the Experience

As you leave Bocas del Toro, take a minute to express your thanks for the experience. Be grateful for the spectacular sunsets that painted the sky in shades of orange and pink, for the warm grins of the people who greeted you with open arms, and for the moments of pure joy as you succumbed to the island rhythm. Remember the friendships you formed, the fun you shared, and the experiences you had together. These memories will keep you happy and inspired long after you leave Bocas del Toro.

Until we meet Again!

As you board your aircraft or boat and say goodbye to Bocas del Toro, remember that it is not goodbye, but hasta luego - until we meet again. Whether you return in a year, a decade, or a lifetime, Bocas del Toro will always greet you with open arms, eager to embrace you in its warmth and beauty once more.

So, when you travel home, bring with you the memories, experiences, and spirit of Bocas del Toro. And remember that while the journey may be done, the charm of Bocas del Toro will linger on in your heart forever. Until we meet again, my traveler, goodbye to paradise.

Glossary of Local Terms and Phrases

Welcome to Bocas del Toro, where the sun shines brightly, the waves move to the beat of the Caribbean, and the residents speak their own language. As you begin on your voyage in this tropical paradise, it's critical to become acquainted with the distinctive terminology and phrases that define the local vernacular. Learn how to speak like a Bocatoreño, from greetings to praise.

1. Bocatoreño or Bocatoreña: (noun) A Bocas del Toro native. Experience the rich local culture and embrace your inner Bocatoreño or Bocatoreña.

2. Mola: (noun) A traditional textile art style used by the Guna indigenous people of Panama and Colombia. Molas are beautifully woven from layers of multicolored cloth, depicting images from nature, mythology, and everyday life.

3. Pura Vida: (phrase) Meaning "pure life," pura vida is a common word in Bocas del Toro and across Central America. It symbolizes the region's relaxed, easygoing spirit and is commonly used as a greeting or farewell.

4. Playa: (noun) Spanish for "beach," playa is a term you'll hear frequently in Bocas del Toro. Whether you're resting on

Playa Bluff or surfing the waves at Playa Paunch, there are plenty of beautiful beaches to explore.

5. Maracuyá: (Noun) Maracuyá, often known as passion fruit, is a tropical fruit that originated in South America. During your visit to Bocas del Toro, try its sweet and tangy flavors in refreshing juices, drinks, and sweets.

6. Chicha: (noun) A traditional fermented beverage produced from maize, chicha is widely consumed in Panama and across Latin America. While it is less widespread in Bocas del Toro than in other locations, handmade versions can be found in rural areas.

7. Panga (noun): A tiny motorized boat that is widely used to carry people between the Bocas del Toro islands. Board a panga for a picturesque cruise to remote beaches, snorkeling areas, and secret coves.

8. Pintxo (noun): A tasty snack made of a tiny piece of bread covered with cheese, meat, fish, or vegetables. Pintxos are a prominent culinary tradition in Bocas del Toro, frequently served as appetizers or finger snacks.

9. Guaymí: The Guaymí people are one of Panama's major indigenous communities with a rich cultural legacy. While visiting Bocas del Toro, take advantage of the chance to learn about their traditions, customs, and way of life.

10. "Que chevere!" (phrase): The word "que chevere!" can convey enthusiasm, adoration, or satisfaction. So go ahead, use it lavishly while you discover everything Bocas del Toro has to offer.

11. Paseo (Noun): Paseo, or leisurely stroll or walk, is a favorite hobby in Bocas del Toro. Whether you're strolling along the coastal promenade or visiting Bocas Town's colorful streets, take a paseo and enjoy the scenery.

12. Gallo Pinto: A classic meal made of rice and beans cooked together and seasoned with onions, peppers, and spices. Gallo pinto is a mainstay of Panamanian cuisine, generally served as a substantial morning meal with eggs, cheese, and fried plantains.

13. Bienvendio/Bienvendia (phrase): Spanish for "welcome," bienvendio (for males) and bienvendia (for ladies) are friendly greetings commonly heard in Bocas del Toro. When you arrive at a hotel, restaurant, or shop, expect to be greeted with a cheerful bienvendio by the locals.

14. Caribeño/Caribeña (noun): The word "caribeño" (for males) and "caribeña" (for ladies) depict the diverse culture of Bocas del Toro. Experience the laid-back, tropical feelings of the Caribbean by connecting with your inner caribeño/caribeña.

15. Panamanismo: (noun): Panamanismo is a distinct part of Panamanian culture or identity that includes anything from traditional practices and festivities to terminology and culinary traditions. Immerse yourself in the panamanismo of Bocas del Toro and learn what makes this location so unique.

Congratulations! You now understand the fundamentals of speaking like a native in Bocas del Toro. Armed with these distinctive terminology and phrases, you'll be able to confidently and stylishly traverse the lively streets, beaches, and rainforests of this tropical paradise. So embrace the local culture and enjoy everything Bocas del Toro has to offer. Pura Vida!

Made in United States
North Haven, CT
22 December 2024

63281891R00104